The Complete Phonemic Awareness Handbook

More Than 300 Playful Activities for Early Reading Success

Anthony D. Fredericks

Illustrated by Dave Garbot

Rigby Best Teachers Press

An imprint of Rigby

Dedication

To Jane Piepmeier, who brings a love of life and a love of learning to all her students—
and everyone with whom she works

For more information about other books from Rigby Best Teachers Press, please contact
Rigby at 800 822-8661 or **www.rigby.com**

Editor: Roberta Dempsey
Executive Editor: Laura Strom
Designer: Biner Design
Design Project Manager: Tom Sjoerdsma
Cover Illustrator: Dave Garbot
Interior Illustrator: Dave Garbot

06 05 04 03
10 9 8 7 6 5 4 3

Printed in the United States of America.

ISBN 0-7635-7347-7 Steck-Vaughn 0-7578-5491-5 Rigby
The Complete Phonemic Awareness Handbook

PreFaCe

ONE OF MY FAVORITE "Far Side" cartoons by Gary Larson shows a group of students in a classroom. One student is raising his hand. He asks, "Mr. Osborne, may I be excused? My brain is full." I like that cartoon for several reasons, but most of all because it illustrates the fun that can be had with learning. Although Larson frequently gave education and teachers a gentle "jab," he also demonstrated how much education is a part of everyday life, too.

I, too, think learning can be fun. I also believe that learning to read can be one of the most exciting subjects of the elementary curriculum. A major impetus for the creation of this book was the fact that children often lack the necessary prerequisites for reading success—prerequisites that can be provided through a fun-filled and engaging program of language play.

When I was growing up in southern California, our home was filled with a plethora of books on every subject. When I got my first flashlight as a kid, I crawled under the covers at night to read the latest Hardy Boys mystery or Tarzan adventure. My teachers at St. Matthew's School in Pacific Palisades made reading a high priority in every subject and every grade. My parents were readers too; they subscribed to magazines and book clubs, were ardent readers of the *Los Angeles Times*, and shared what they learned during dinner table conversations. The enchantment of reading was a constant in our household. (I suspect that this literate background was a major impetus in my decision to become a teacher.)

As an educator for more than 30 years, I have tried to share the joy and excitement of reading with my own students. In my role as a classroom teacher and reading specialist, I worked to fill my room with literature and my students' lives with the skills and abilities to participate actively in, and become engaged by, that literature. I also wanted to provide my students with a wealth of opportunities to experience language in all its forms—reading, listening, singing, storytelling, writing, and speaking. In fact, it was well known that my first graders and I could out-sing any classroom in the school.

(It's an equally well-known fact that I cannot carry a tune to save my soul, so our renditions of "Old MacDonald Had a Farm" and "The Itsy Bitsy Spider" would not only bring gladness to the heart of my principal but could just as easily bring tears to his eyes!)

The ideas in this book sprang from my own experiences as a student constantly surrounded by books and my work as a classroom teacher helping children develop a working knowledge of how language works. This book also grew out of conversations with fellow educators around the country who were looking for an all-inclusive resource that would help ensure that the prerequisites of reading success could be provided in a stimulating classroom environment.

The Complete Phonemic Awareness Handbook has been designed as an easy-to-use resource guide for the busy classroom teacher. While the emphasis is on the *playful* aspects of language, the message is that knowledge of the sounds of language—as well as the manipulation of those sounds—is a necessary and essential component of future reading success. The more than 300 phonemic awareness activities included within these pages have all been enthusiastically implemented in a variety of primary classrooms from coast to coast. They have been embraced by teachers, celebrated by parents, and shared by students with remarkable success.

I sincerely hope that you and your students discover the fun and excitement of language learning within the pages of this book. May your classroom be filled with happiness, song, laughter, stories, and, most important, the love of learning!

Tony Fredericks

AcknOwLedgMents

THIS BOOK WOULD not have been possible without the support and dedication of several individuals.

To two of the most talented and creative teachers I know—Joanne Nosoff and Christine Buffone—I give a standing ovation, a thunderous applause, and a crescendo of cheers. Their expertise was instrumental in generating a plethora of engaging and dynamic activities. Their students are truly fortunate to be the recipients of their ingenuity, skill, and sensitivity.

To Pam Garfield of the Arcadia (CA) Unified School District, whose review of the initial manuscript was both insightful as well as perceptive, I extend my heartiest appreciation. Her clear-sighted comments and sage suggestions were pivotal in shaping and clarifying specific elements of this book. It was both a privilege and honor to work with her on this project.

To my longtime friend and editor, Bobbie Dempsey, I send along lots of hugs, loads of gratitude, and tons of admiration. Bobbie is truly the "best of the best," and she makes every book project an exciting adventure and an extraordinary experience.

To Laura Strom, who made the phone call inviting me to join the Rigby family, I am forever indebted. Her belief in this project and her faith in this writer are truly appreciated. I am honored to be part of the team.

CoNtents

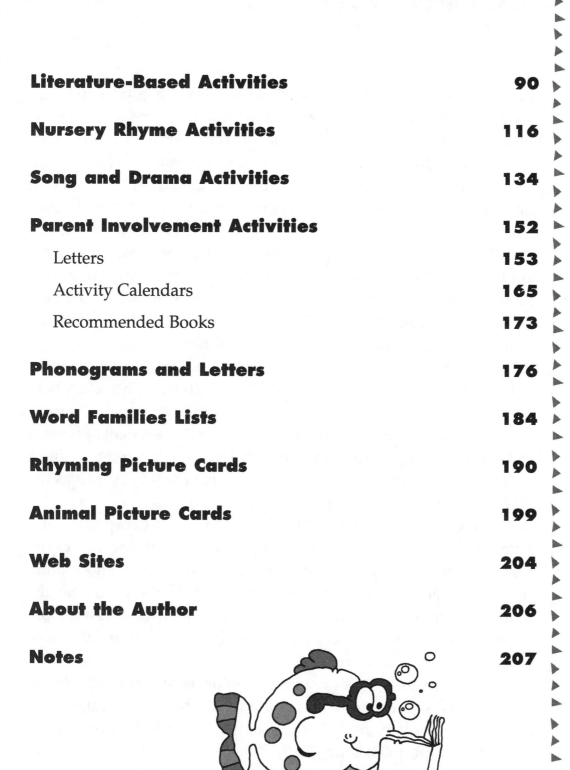

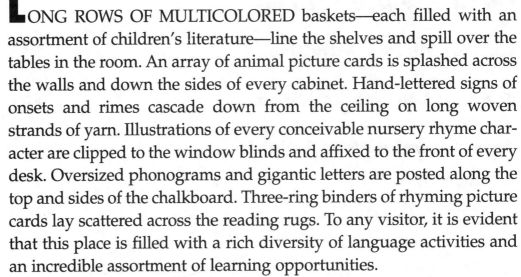

INTRODUCTION

LONG ROWS OF MULTICOLORED baskets—each filled with an assortment of children's literature—line the shelves and spill over the tables in the room. An array of animal picture cards is splashed across the walls and down the sides of every cabinet. Hand-lettered signs of onsets and rimes cascade down from the ceiling on long woven strands of yarn. Illustrations of every conceivable nursery rhyme character are clipped to the window blinds and affixed to the front of every desk. Oversized phonograms and gigantic letters are posted along the top and sides of the chalkboard. Three-ring binders of rhyming picture cards lay scattered across the reading rugs. To any visitor, it is evident that this place is filled with a rich diversity of language activities and an incredible assortment of learning opportunities.

Caroline Lourie has been a first-grade teacher in northern California for the last seven years. Visitors entering her classroom often feel as though they have been transported "through the looking glass" to a world filled with every conceivable element of written and spoken language. Caroline has transformed her classroom into a wonderland awash in the sights and sounds of words as well as the playfulness inherent in language learning.

Caroline knows that her students need a solid background and a strong understanding of spoken language before they can comprehend written language. She also realizes that her students' future success in reading is highly dependent on their ability to hear the sounds that make up words, their ability to understand the relationships between those sounds, and their ability to manipulate those sounds to create new words.

Caroline is part of a growing legion of classroom teachers who recognize the significance and importance of phonemic awareness as a foundation for later reading success (Juel, Griffith, & Gough, 1986; Griffith & Olson, 1992; Yopp, 1999). This belief is built on three statements that we know to be absolutely true about the reading process:

1. Words are made up of sounds.

2. The ability to hear and manipulate individual sounds is called *phonemic awareness.*

3. Phonemic awareness, along with letter recognition, is the best indicator of future reading success.

That last statement is not a haphazard one. It is based on years of research about how children learn and especially about how children learn to read (Lundberg, Frost, & Petersen, 1988; Adams, 1990; Griffith, Klesius, & Kromrey, 1992; Stanovich, 1994). Scores of classroom teachers and university researchers have conclusively and emphatically proven that an awareness of the sounds of language is both necessary and essential to success with print. Implied within that statement is the inescapable fact that *if young children are provided with systematic instruction in phonemic awareness, they will be better prepared for printed language.*

What Is Phonemic Awareness?

Phonemic awareness instruction provides children with opportunities to experience spoken language before they start to learn written language. The ability to hear and manipulate sounds is referred to as *phonemic awareness.* Implicit in this definition is the fact that children need to hear the sounds of language (for example, "Hickory, Dickory, *Dock*; the mouse ran up the *Clock*"). Hearing the sounds of words is completely independent of the meaning of those words (a skill that is developed later in the reading process). It is also important for children to identify the sequence of sounds within an oral unit (what we call a *word*; for example, "What is the last sound you hear in the word *book*?"). Third, phonemic awareness is the ability of children to understand the relationship that phonemes play in word formation (for example, "Let's take the sound /s/ and add it to the sound /at/. What word do we have?").

The importance of phonemic awareness lies in the fact that it lets children know that language can be manipulated. By combining sounds, subtracting sounds, and rearranging sounds, we can create elements known as *words*. It is these words that help us communicate with each other. For young children the path to that communication begins with the ability to hear the sounds in words, the various positions of those sounds within one or more words, and an understanding of the role of those sounds within a single word. As such, phonemic awareness is a sequenced series of oral language skills that precede a child's transition into written language.

It is important to understand that phonemic awareness does not just "happen." Phonemic awareness is a sequential and developmental process. Certain abilities precede others and must be mastered before other skills can be learned. Forming a strong foundation in phonemic awareness abilities is a precursor to the foundation of reading skills that takes place later in the reading process. Following is a sequential ordering of phonemic awareness abilities children need to acquire:

1. Awareness of spoken words (we can communicate orally via logical units of speech).

2. Many words have similar or matching sounds (words can rhyme with each other).

3. Many words begin with the same sound (alliteration; for example, "Tommy's toy turtle is on the table.").

4. Words have syllables (words can be divided into distinct parts).

5. Words have onsets (the sounds of a word that come before the first vowel).

6. Words have rimes (the first vowel in a word and all the sounds that follow).

7. The sounds in a word appear in specific locations (each sound has a specific position, such as beginning, middle, end).

8. Words have individual sounds (consonants and vowels have one or more different sounds).

9. The sounds of a word can be separated (a word can be divided into its component phonemes, for example, "Can you tell me the three sounds in the word *mouse*?" [/m/ /ow/ /s/])

10. The sounds of a word can be manipulated (beginning, middle, and ending sounds in a word can be replaced with other beginning, middle, and ending sounds; also, beginning, middle, and ending sounds can be eliminated from a word).

Instruction in phonemic awareness provides young children with multiple opportunities to "experience" oral language. As a result, children begin to understand, use, and apply oral language in a host of situations. They develop proficiencies in the appreciation, utility, and manipulation of language that help solidify an understanding of how language "works." This understanding is the foundation upon which written language abilities are based. It is also the foundation for phonics instruction and later, for reading instruction.

Phonemic Awareness and Phonics

It is important to understand that there is a difference between phonemic awareness and phonics. Phonemic awareness deals with the sounds in spoken language, while phonics involves the relationship between spoken sounds (phonemes) and written symbols (graphemes). In other words, phonemic awareness instruction focuses on the oral aspects of words—the sounds that letters and letter combinations make. Phonics is the next logical element in the developmental nature of reading acquisition, since it is at this level that children learn the sound-print relationships of words. In short, phonemic awareness precedes phonics. Or, to state it another way, success in phonics, spelling, word recognition, reading, and writing skills is dependent upon a solid foundation of phonemic awareness skills (Juel, 1988; Griffith & Olson, 1992; Yopp, 1992).

Phonemic Awareness:	**Phonics:**
A recognition that spoken words are composed of several individual sounds. Focuses on sound units (phonemes).	A recognition of sound-spelling relationships in printed words. Associates sounds (phonemes) to written symbols (graphemes).

It is also important to keep in mind that phonemic awareness and phonics are not mutually exclusive, but rather mutually dependent. Before children can understand sound-symbol relationships (phonics), they must be able to hear and manipulate oral sound patterns (phonemic awareness). Phonics builds upon the foundation established earlier in a child's educational "career" in which she or he has developed the ability to hear sounds and segment and blend those sounds together in a wide variety of oral tasks. In other words, without sufficient exposure to phonemic awareness tasks, many children will have considerable difficulty in mastering essential decoding (phonics) skills.

Unfortunately, many children come to school without an adequate background of phonemic awareness. They have not been exposed to the rhymes, rhythms, songs, sounds, patterns, or fun of oral language. As a reading specialist, I often worked with kindergarten teachers to develop a series of "remedial Mother Goose" experiences for children. (Sorry, photos of me in my Mother Goose costume are no longer available . . . thank goodness!) These activities were designed to expose children to the rhymes of language that had been lacking in their home environments. Interestingly, there is current evidence that as much as 20 percent of children entering school lack any exposure to phonemic awareness activities (such as playing with the sounds of language), and that number may be growing.

Phonemic Awareness and Reading Development

The relationship between phonemic awareness and reading instruction is considerable. Without proficiency in phonemic awareness, children may not have the necessary foundation for later reading competency. Numerous classroom studies have conclusively supported these two seemingly contradictory facts: 1) phonemic awareness is a necessary prerequisite for learning to read, and 2) phonemic awareness is a consequence of learning to read (Ehri, 1979; Perfetti, Beck, Bell, & Hughes, 1987; Tunmer, Herriman, & Nesdale, 1988; Yopp, 1992). What that means is that exposure to the oral sounds of language helps prepare children for dealing with the written forms of language. Concomitantly, by exposing children to the written forms of language, their appreciation of oral language is heightened considerably.

I like to think of this relationship in a cyclical way; that is, the more children are exposed to the sounds and rhythms of language, the better they will be in dealing with written forms of language. And the more children are exposed to the forms of written language, the more they appreciate the oral foundations of that language. In a real sense, it's a mutually supportive and integrative way of looking at language development: each supports and reinforces the other.

But, just like any journey, that cycle must have a beginning, and that beginning is an understanding on the part of children (such as pre-readers) that speech (how we communicate with one another in an oral format) is composed of a series of individual sounds. An enormous body of research indicates that one of the best predictors of early reading success is phonemic awareness. In fact, there is convincing evidence that awareness of the sounds of language is a far better predictor of future literacy development than is I.Q. or vocabulary (Stanovich, 1994).

Indeed, much of the research on the value of phonemic awareness instruction and its relationship to reading can be boiled down to the following statement:

> Children who receive phonemic awareness training in preschool, kindergarten, and first grade do significantly better on *all* measures of formal reading achievement (*throughout* their educational career) when compared with children who do not receive such training.

What becomes abundantly clear from an enormous body of reading research is that children who have difficulty in learning to read or who have failed to learn to read are those who also lack phonemic awareness abilities. Equally clear is the fact that phonemic awareness is a precursor for later reading success and forms the foundation upon which young children can begin to develop (and appreciate) early literacy skills.

Teaching Phonemic Awareness

Phonemic awareness activities should establish a sense of "comfortableness" with the oral sounds of language. They should be designed to enhance children's experiences with spoken language—hearing and recognizing certain sounds, identifying and understanding the way sounds are sequenced in words, and noting and learning about the role of phonemes in word construction.

Here are some points you may wish to consider in developing an appropriate program of phonemic awareness activities:

1. Phonemic awareness occurs in five separate, yet progressive stages (see page 18). Children need to achieve a level of familiarity and assurance in one stage before progressing to the next stage. It is very important to understand, however, that children *do not need to establish complete competency in one stage before being introduced to the next successive stage* of phonemic awareness activities. What is important here is that children are *exposed* to earlier phonemic awareness activities (such as Stage 1 and Stage 2), before they are *exposed* to later activities (such as Stage 4 and Stage 5). In fact, several sections of this book (for example, the Nursery Rhyme Activities and Song and Drama Activities) incorporate activities from multiple stages so that children can experience a wide range of playful and instructive phonemic awareness opportunities. In so doing, children will learn to appreciate the interrelationships that can and do exist between and among the various stages.

2. Feedback from a host of classroom teachers has shown that instruction in phonemic awareness does not have to be intensive in order to be effective. Fifteen to 20 minutes a day over a period of 20 to 25 weeks is one suggested model. The number of weeks of instruction is not important; what is more important is that the length of each instructional period not exceed 20 minutes. This is simply because the attention span of young children cannot handle concentrated instructional activities in one area for more than that time frame. Also, phonemic awareness instruction should be but one element (albeit, a most important element) in an overall literacy program.

3. Instruction in phonemic awareness achieves its greatest potency when it is part of a balanced literacy program. In other words, phonemic awareness instruction should not be "divorced" from other literacy activities (such as reading aloud, listening games, storytelling, "show and tell," informal talk activities, creative dramatics, and puppetry). In fact, there will be many opportunities during the course of the day to draw parallels and/or comparisons between phonemic awareness tasks and other elements of your reading/language arts program. For example:

"Doesn't this word (in a read-aloud book) rhyme with a word we heard earlier today?"

"Ramone, you used a word in show and tell that began with the same sound as a word we learned earlier today."

"Catherine, you said a sound that we wrote and placed on the chalkboard tray. Can you find that sound?"

"Here's the same word we saw earlier today. Let's take off the beginning sound just like we did this morning."

4. One question that is always in the mind of any learner (from preschool through college) is "Why do I have to learn this?" It is important to share with children the reasons why they are engaged in phonemic awareness activities. You may wish to say, "These activities will help us in learning to read," or "We need to learn sounds so that we can learn letters." The exact wording of the statements is not critical; what is more important is that children understand how and why these activities are important for reading.

5. Make children's literature a regular extension of your phonemic awareness activities. Reading aloud to children from quality books not only stimulates their imaginations, enhances their listening skills, and introduces them to a wide variety of reading experiences; so too, does it provide a forum for "learning in context." The inclusion of literature introduces children to the sounds of language, the patterns of language, and the natural relationship that exists between oral and written language. In other words, children can hear the sounds they are learning about in authentic contexts, and can begin to understand that wonderful connection between learning about sounds and using those sounds in meaningful ways.

6. Since many of the activities throughout this book incorporate various phonemic awareness stages, it is important to note that they can be used to meet the instructional needs of a variety of children in your classroom. You will discover activities and projects for both ESL (English as a Second Language) learners and children with learning disabilities. The utility of these activities ensures that you can offer differentiated instruction for a diversity of learners and learning situations.

Training in phonemic awareness does not have to be formalized to be effective. Rather, it should be perceived by children as a natural and normal part of the overall instructional program, just as much as it should be viewed as a natural and normal (and fun) part of everyday life.

References

Adams, M. J. (1990). *Beginning to read: Thinking and learning about print.* Cambridge, MA: MIT Press.

Ehri, L. (1979). "Linguistic insight: Threshold of reading acquisition." In T. Waller & G. MacKinnon (Eds.), *Reading research: Advances in theory and practice* (Vol. 1, pp. 63–114). New York: Academic Press.

Griffith, P., Klesius, J., & Kromrey, J. (1992). "The effect of phonemic awareness on the literacy development of first-grade children in a traditional or a whole language classroom." *Journal of Research in Childhood Education, 6,* 86–92.

Griffith, P., & Olson, M. (1992). "Phonemic awareness helps beginning readers break the code." *The Reading Teacher, 45,* 516–523.

Juel, C. (1988). "Learning to read and write: A longitudinal study of 54 children from first through fourth grades." *Journal of Educational Psychology*, 80, 437–447.

Juel, C., Griffith, P., & Gough, P. (1986). "Acquisition of literacy: A longitudinal study of children in first and second grade." *Journal of Educational Psychology*, 78, 243–255.

Lundberg, I., Frost, J., & Petersen, O. (1988). "Effects of an extensive program for stimulating phonological awareness in preschool children." *Reading Research Quarterly*, 23, 263–285.

Perfetti, C., Beck, I., Bell, L., & Hughes, C. (1987). "Phonemic knowledge and learning to read are reciprocal: A longitudinal study of first-grade children." *Merrill-Palmer Quarterly*, 33, 283–319.

Stanovich, K. (1994). "Romance and reason." *The Reading Teacher*, 47, 280–291.

Tunmer, W., Herriman, M., & Nesdale, A. (1988). "Metalinguistic abilities and beginning reading." *Reading Research Quarterly*, 23, 159–177.

Yopp, H. (1992). "Developing phonemic awareness in young children." *The Reading Teacher*, 45, 696–703.

Yopp, H. (1999). "Phonemic awareness: Frequently asked questions." *The California Reader*, 32, 21–27.

ThE StaGes of PhoNemic AwaRenEss

THE ACTIVITIES IN THIS BOOK are organized into five separate yet interrelated stages. It is assumed that students will be exposed to earlier stages before exposure to later stages. Knowledge of these stages will assist you in organizing and presenting appropriate phonemic awareness activities for all students in your class.

Stage 1: Rhyming and Alliteration
Stage 2: Word Parts
Stage 3: Sound Positions
Stage 4: Sound Separation
Stage 5: Sound Manipulation

Sample Activity

I will say some sentences that have two words that rhyme. After I say each sentence, I will say it again, but I'll leave off the last word. You tell me a rhyming word we could use at the end of each sentence:

- One is for fun.
- One is for _____.
- Two is for blue.
- Two is for _____.
- Three is for me.
- Three is for _____.
- Four is for door.
- Four is for _____.
- Five is for drive.
- Five is for _____.

Stage 1: Rhyming and Alliteration

At this initial stage of phonemic awareness, the focus is primarily on helping children hear and appreciate the rhyming and alliterative nature of selected words. The intent is to assist children in developing appropriate auditory discrimination skills that help them notice the similarities that exist between and among selected words.

Rhyming tasks are those to which children gravitate naturally (such as poetry, nursery rhymes, and songs) simply because they illustrate the fun that can be had with words. Important in sharing the rhythmic nature of comparable sounds is that early in their exposure to phonemic awareness, children get a sense that language play is not didactic in nature, but rather is creative, imaginative, and fun.

Also implicit at this stage is the notion that much of the English language is filled with similarities. For example, there are word patterns that are similar (rhyming) and there are sounds that come at the beginning of many words that are similar, too (alliteration). In effect, children begin to hear and understand the similarities that exist between and among words. It is these similarities that help them interconnect and appreciate the sounds in words.

Stage 2: Word Parts

In the first stage of phonemic awareness, children become attuned to the gross similarities between and among words—the fact that words are composed of sounds and that these sounds have similar features or characteristics. In Stage 2 children move to the next logical step in their awareness of spoken language: they begin to listen for sound units within words. While this process is logical and comprehensible for adults, it marks a major "cognitive leap" for children. In the first stage, children deal with whole words. The implication for many young children is that single words comprise single sounds.

In the second stage of development, children begin to make some amazing discoveries. First of all, words can be divided into more than one sound and these sounds occur in a particular sequence (beginning sound + ending sound). These units of sound are known as *onsets* (sound units that occur at the beginning of a word, before a vowel) and *rimes* (sound units that occur at the end of words and include a vowel). For example, the word *green* has an onset (*gr-*) and a rime (*-een*).

This stage also provides children with an awareness of *syllables*. Syllables are simply another way of dividing words into their component parts. Syllabication is a conventional way of breaking a word into phonetic elements we call syllables. For most words, a syllable is defined as the smallest unit of speech with a vowel sound. For example, the word *snowman* has two syllables, *snow* (one vowel sound, /ow/) and *man* (one vowel sound, /a/).

Sample Activity

I'm going to say some sounds very slowly. Listen very carefully, put all the sounds together, and tell me the word you hear each time:

/n/ /o/
/i/ /t/
/s/ /o/

Let's do it again. This time, I'll say some new sounds very slowly. Put them together and tell me the word you hear each time:

/f/ /r/ /o/ /g/
/g/ /oo/ /d/
/h/ /e/ /l/ /p/

Third, this stage provides children with exposure to phonemes, the individual sounds that correspond to individual letters or graphemes. For example, the word *dog* has three phonemes, which are blended together: /d/ + /o/ + /g/.

What is most important at this stage is for children to understand that words are "blended sounds." There are many different kinds of sounds in the English language, and when we take two or more of those sounds and "put them together," we can create something known as a word. In other words, sound units are combined to form words. Thoroughly understanding the concept of sound blending (Stage 2) is critical to a later and more complex concept—dividing words into their sound units (Stage 4).

Sample Activity

I would like to have Tara, Michael, and Luis stand in the front of the room. Tara will be first in line, Michael will be in the middle, and Luis will be the last in line. I will say a word that you all know. Then, I will ask Tara, Michael, and Luis to tell us where they heard certain sounds in that word. The word is *boat*.

Tara, what was the *first* sound you heard in the word *boat*? (/b/)

Michael, what was the *middle* sound you heard in the word *boat*? (/oa/)

Luis, what was the *ending* sound you heard in the word *boat*? (/t/)

Boys and girls, notice that Tara had the first sound and she was first in line, Michael had the middle sound and he was the middle person in line, and Luis had the ending sound and he was at the end of the line.

Stage 3: Sound Positions

This particular stage of phonemic awareness is what I like to call the "bridge stage," because it helps children develop a very important and critical bridge between knowledge of sounds in a word and the position of those sounds. For many children words are often viewed as a "mishmash" of sounds. Many children often perceive a word as one big sound or hear that as a hodgepodge of randomly assembled sounds without order or sequence.

At this stage children are exposed to the positional nature of individual sounds within a word, that is, what sound comes at the *beginning* of a word, what sound comes in the *middle* of a word, and what sound comes at the *end* of a word. In other words, each sound within a word has a specific (and logical) *position* within that word. Essential to the success of instruction at this stage is that children have prior knowledge about positional words and what they mean. Children must understand words such as *before*, *beginning*, and *first*. They also need to comprehend words such

as *end, ending,* and *last.* Knowledge of such words as *middle* and *in between* is also important.

It is not essential that children know the names of the letters of the alphabet for this stage to be successful. This particular stage is also a precursor to later instruction in letter recognition. As in the previous two stages, children are still being exposed to the sounds of language (phonemes). Instruction in the written elements of language (graphemes) typically occurs later in the instructional sequence.

Stage 4: Sound Separation

This stage of phonemic awareness is one of the most challenging for many children, simply because it seems to be an illogical task. In Stage 2 children are asked to blend sounds together in order to form comprehensible units we know as words. It is these words that humans use to communicate with each other. This "sequencing" of tasks makes sense to children because the final "product" (a word) is something that they use and understand.

In Stage 4, however, children are asked to do the reverse of what they learned in Stage 2. In this stage the individual sounds within a word are identified. In other words, children move from the whole to the parts (in Stage 2 they moved from the parts to the whole, a more logical sequence). Stage 4 activities require children to separate the sounds in a word, a task that is frequently complex and difficult for many young learners. You may wish to explain to children that these activities will help them learn to spell later.

Also included in this stage of phonemic awareness are activities that provide opportunities for children to count the number of phonemes within a word. It is often recommended that these types of activities precede activities that focus on identifying individual sounds. Identifying the number of sounds within a word is a simpler task than identifying the actual sounds within that word.

Sample Activity

I would like everyone to stand up. I will say some words to you one at a time. Then, I will say each word again very slowly. When you hear the first sound in each word, put your hands on your head. When you hear the middle sound in each word, put your hands on your waist. When you hear the ending sound in each word, put your hands on your toes. Ready?

kite–/k/ (head), /i/ (waist), /t/ (toes)

three–/th/ (head), /r/ (waist), /e/ (toes)

yes–/y/ (head), /e/ (waist), /s/ (toes)

red–/r/ (head), /e/ (waist), /d/ (toes)

make–/m/ (head), /a/ (waist), /k/ (toes)

Stage 5: Sound Manipulation

The final stage of phonemic awareness can be the most playful of all. It is at this stage that children are provided with numerous opportunities to manipulate, rearrange, resequence, and reconfigure the sounds using skills they have learned in the previous four stages. Children can add sounds to words, delete sounds from other words, rearrange sounds in some words to create new words, and move sounds around to invent new formations. With a solid foundation in the first four stages, children will appreciate the "playfulness" of language inherent throughout this stage. This stage comprises two levels. The first level provides opportunities for children to delete sounds from a word. Present children with activities that focus first on the deletion of beginning sounds (typically consonants), then ending sounds (also consonants), and finally middle sounds.

The second level involves the substitution of sounds in a word in order to create a new word or sound unit. As is the previous level, children should initially substitute sounds at the beginning of words, then at the end of words, and finally in the middle of words. The focus of this stage is on the playful nature of language. That is, language is never static; rather, it provides learners (of any age) with a multitude of opportunities to manipulate sounds in creative and fascinating ways.

Sample Activity

Let's do some riddles. For each riddle, I'll give you a sound and a word. You add the sound to the beginning of the word to create a brand new word. Here we go!

Add /m/ to *ice* to make the word _____.

Add /b/ to *old* to make the word _____.

Add /g/ to *oat* to make the word _____.

Add /s/ to *eat* to make the word _____.

Add /r/ to *at* to make the word _____.

The sequence of stages listed here is presented in order of difficulty. That is, most children will find that rhyming activities will be considerably easier to master than those that involve the manipulation of phonetic elements. While it might seem logical to have children master one task type completely before moving on to the next, that's not necessary nor is it always possible. Providing students with a "mix" of phonemic awareness activities will keep interest levels high and expose children to a wide variety of "sounding" opportunities in a host of positive learning endeavors.

How to Use This Book

THE SUCCESS OF YOUR phonemic awareness program will revolve around regular, systematic, and sustained activities naturally incorporated into your daily classroom curriculum. As mentioned earlier, phonemic awareness instruction should be but one element in an overall literacy program. The activities in this book are designed to offer you a plethora of possibilities and opportunities for engaging children in the playfulness of language. Here are some ideas:

- Phonemic awareness activities should be a regular and daily occurrence. There is significant evidence to support the notion that about 15 to 20 minutes per day is sufficient for most children.

- Keep the emphasis on informality and playfulness. You may wish to assign this part of the school day a special name (for example, "Fun with Language Time," "Playing with Sounds," "Sound Off," or "Hear, Hear").

- Administer the Phonemic Awareness Assessment instrument (page 26) early in the academic year. This will provide you with valuable data upon which to structure subsequent activities and projects.

- Be aware of the five stages of phonemic awareness. Provide activities appropriate to each individual's level of development.

- By the same token, children need to be exposed to a wide variety of phonemic awareness activities. You may wish to emphasize the activities at one stage of development for a group of children while also introducing them to activities from other stages.

- A "mix" of various activities within a selected stage and across different stages is appropriate for most children. Be aware of individual needs (see the Phonemic Awareness Assessment on page 26), but also be aware that a variety of experiences is important too.

- Listen carefully to the language used by children in everyday situations. Take advantage of that language and incorporate it into your own phonemic awareness activities.

- Keep in mind that the activities and suggestions throughout this book can be viewed as generic in nature. In short, please feel free to use your own words, the words of children in your classroom, or words from a district or state-mandated list. Even better, plan regular opportunities to utilize words from the stories and literature you share with children each day.

- Provide and promote activities that encourage interaction among children. The best phonemic awareness activities are group-based.

- Many activities invite children to cut and paste photographs from old magazines. As an alternative, consider buying simply illustrated primary coloring books. These will have larger uncomplicated pictures that children can identify.

- As an organizational aid, consider photocopying the various sets of cards in this book on different colored paper. For example, duplicate the Rhyming Picture Cards on blue card stock; the Animal Picture Cards on yellow card stock; and the Phonograms and Letters on green card stock. In addition, use colored index cards (blue, yellow, green) to categorize pasted magazine pictures.

- Phonemic awareness programs can also be informal programs. In other words, don't just limit phonemic awareness to a specific time of the day, but rather take advantage of the unplanned and informal opportunities that arise naturally (those "teachable moments"). Times when children line up for lunch, story time, indoor recess, and "Show and Tell" time are but a few of the many opportunities you'll have to include some playful language activities.

- It's important for children to hear the sounds of language in natural contexts. Use children's literature as a way to introduce and emphasize phonemic awareness in an authentic way. Read to children regularly, stopping every so often to note the sounds in a word, the alliteration of letters, funny or unusual rhymes, or a distinctive arrangement of syllables. The trade books you normally share with children can be positive components of your phonemic awareness program.

- It's not essential that you use all the activities within a designated stage in this book. Keep in mind, however, that the activities and suggestions within a stage are sequenced according to their level of difficulty. Thus, early activities (such as activities 1, 2, or 3) will be easier for children to participate in than activities that occur later (such as activities 10, 11, or 12).

All of the activities in this book have been classroom-tested and "kid-tested." All are designed to offer you and your students some wonderful adventures and exciting discoveries about the sounds of language. Make them a regular part of your phonemic awareness program, modify them according to the specific needs of children in your classroom, and add to them via the ideas and suggestions that naturally occur in any preschool, kindergarten, or first grade classroom. Keep the emphasis on *playfulness*, and you're sure to see some delightful learning taking place.

PhoNemic AwaRenEss AssEssMent

THE FOLLOWING ASSESSMENT instrument is designed to help you determine the appropriate stage of phonemic awareness development for individual students in your classroom. It is not designed as a group or class test, but rather an instrument that will assist you in targeting instruction for individual students.

- Administer the Assessment in an oral format, one child at a time. The actual administration will take approximately 10 minutes per child and an entire class can be assessed in less than a week (depending on your schedule of regular activities).

- It may not be appropriate or necessary to assess every child in the class. Some children will have sufficient phonetic skills that will preclude them from this assessment process.

- It is not necessary to "go through" the entire test with every child. Some children will indicate early stages of phonemic awareness development (such as rhyming), but will become frustrated when attempting later stages (for example, sound positions). Use your judgment in stopping the testing process at an appropriate point. This is always preferable to "forcing" a child through a complete assessment procedure.

- Following the test is an Assessment Grid (page 33) that allows you to record the names of the children down the left-hand side. The phonemic awareness skills are listed across the top of the grid. You can then check each box in which a child meets the standard. Empty boxes will indicate children who can be easily grouped together for targeted instruction, especially if most of the other children are ready to move ahead.

The information gathered from this instrument will help you decide on the instructional activities and materials needed for individual children as well as the types of cooperative groups that you can form with children of like abilities.

Phonemic Awareness Assessment

Student Name: _____ Date: _____

Test Administrator: _____

Stage 1: Rhyming and Alliteration

Rhyming Identification

Read each pair of words orally. Circle each pair the child correctly identifies. Say: "I will read two words to you. Tell me if the two words rhyme. Here are two words that rhyme: *ball–fall*. Here are two words that don't rhyme: *ball–bat*."

bed–red	crack–pink	pill–grill	tuck–tack
boat–float	nose–close	mail–rake	bank–rice

Rhyming Utility

Read each word orally. Write the word the child supplies on the appropriate space. Say: "I will read a word to you. Tell me another word that rhymes with the first word. Here's an example: *meet–feet*."

nail_____   sick_____   bug_____

bake_____   map_____   cot_____

Alliteration Identification

Read each set of words orally. Circle each set the child correctly identifies. Say: "I will read three words to you. Tell me if the three words all begin with the same sound. Here's an example of three words that all begin with the same sound: *nose, nail, nice*."

set, sail, soar	rub, frog, rack	pen, pat, poke
bun, best, ton	hole, hair, help	gate, goat, goose

Alliteration Utility

Read each pair of words orally. Write the word the child supplies on the appropriate space. Say: "I will read two words to you. Tell me one more word that has the same beginning sound as the first two words. Here's an example: *bank, boy, boat*."

meet, mail, _____   coat, cap, _____

fog, fast, _____   date, deer, _____

nice, nail, _____   tape, tail, _____

Possible Score: 26

Student's Score: _____

Stage 2: Word Parts

Onsets

Say each sound orally. Write the word the child says next to the sound. Say: "I will make the sound of a letter. Tell me a word that begins with that sound. Here's an example: /d/–*dive*."

/s/ _____   /t/ _____
/b/ _____   /m/ _____
/j/ _____   /k/ _____

Rimes

Say each sound orally. Write the word the child says next to the sound. Say: "I will make a sound. Tell me a word that ends with that sound. Here's an example: /ad/–*dad*."

/ed/ _____   /op/ _____
/ing/ _____   /ake/ _____
/ell/ _____   /id/ _____

Syllabication

Say each two-syllable word slowly. Circle each word the child correctly blends. Say: "I'll say a word very slowly. I'll say it in two parts. Put the two parts together and tell me what the word is. Here's an example: *birth . . . day–birthday*."

base . . . ball   fun . . . ny   pop . . . corn
mop . . . ping   sun . . . set   can . . . dy

Phoneme Blending

For each word, say the individual phonemes slowly. Circle each word in which the child correctly blends the phonemes. Say: "I will say some sounds very slowly. Put the sounds together and tell me the word you hear. Here's an example: /b/ /o/ /t/–*boat*."

/i/ /t/   /p/ /e/ /n/   /f/ /r/ /o/ /g/
/s/ /o/   /j/ /um/ /p/   /s/ /t/ /o/ /p/

Possible Score: 24
Student's Score: _____

Stage 3: Sound Positions

Beginning Sounds

Read each word orally to the child. Circle the words the child correctly identifies. Say: "Tell me the sound you hear at the beginning of each word I say to you. Here's an example: *five*–/f/."

say	pail	dice
jump	old	chain

Middle Sounds

Read each word orally to the child. Circle the words the child correctly identifies. Say: "Tell me the sound you hear in the middle of each word I say to you. Here's an example: *chain*–/a/."

green	big	yes
ride	mouse	rack

Ending Sounds

Read each word orally to the child. Circle the words the child correctly identifies. Say: "Tell me the sound you hear at the end of each word I say to you. Here's an example: *pain*–/n/."

top	ride	flat
duck	skill	plum

Possible Score: 18

Student's Score: _____

Stage 4: Sound Separation

Phoneme Counting

Say each word for the child. Circle the words the child correctly identifies. Say: "I will say a word. For each word, tell me how many sounds you hear. Here's an example: In *dig* there are three sounds, /d/ /i/ /g/."

hen (3)   cow (2)   but (3)

horse (3)   this (3)   me (2)

Phoneme Segmentation

Say each word for the child. Circle the words the child correctly identifies. Say: "I will say a word. Then I would like you to say the word back to me very slowly so I can hear each sound in the word. Here's an example: *bell*–/b/ /e/ /l/."

brown   eat   help

truck   pig   gum

Possible Score: 12

Student's Score: _____

Stage 5: Sound Manipulation

Sound Deletion

Say each sentence for the child. Circle the sentence to which the child correctly responds. Say: "I will say a word. Then I will ask you to say the word, but leave off a sound that I tell you. Here's an example: Say *jet* without the /j/–/et/."

Say *bird* without the /b/.
Say *sad* without the /s/.
Say *work* without the /w/.

Say *must* without the /t/.
Say *sleep* without the /p/.
Say *flag* without the /g/.

Say *ball* without the /a/.
Say *run* without the /u/.
Say *well* without the /e/.

Sound Substitution

Say each sentence for the child. Circle the sentence to which the child correctly responds. Say: "I will say a word. Then I will ask you to change something about the word and say it back to me. Here's an example: Take away the first sound in *sell* and replace it with a /f/–*fell*."

Take away the first sound in *hit* and replace it with a /b/.
Take away the first sound in *dog* and replace it with a /f/.
Take away the first sound in *best* and replace it with a /n/.

Take away the last sound in *bug* and replace it with a /t/.
Take away the last sound in *skin* and replace it with a /p/.
Take away the last sound in *rock* and replace it with a /b/.

Take away the middle sound in *cat* and replace it with a /u/.
Take away the middle sound in *bell* and replace it with a /i/.
Take away the middle sound in *tub* and replace it with a /a/.

Possible Score: 18
Student's Score: _____

Phonemic Awareness Assessment Scoring Rubric

Directions: Add up the total number of points for each of the five sections of the Assessment. Using the rubric below, put a check mark in one of the four boxes following the title of each section to indicate the child's score for that section. The column with the most check marks is indicative of the student's overall level of competency in phonemic awareness (Very Competent, Moderately Competent, Minimally Competent, Not Competent).

	Child is very competent	Child is moderately competent	Child is minimally competent	Child is not competent
Rhyming & Alliteration	24–26 ___ points	20–23 ___ points	15–19 ___ points	0–14 ___ points
Word Parts	22–24 ___ points	18–21 ___ points	13–17 ___ points	0–12 ___ points
Sound Positions	16–18 ___ points	12–15 ___ points	8–11 ___ points	0–7 ___ points
Sound Separation	10–12 ___ points	7–9 ___ points	5–6 ___ points	0–4 ___ points
Sound Manipulation	16–18 ___ points	12–15 ___ points	8–11 ___ points	0–7 ___ points

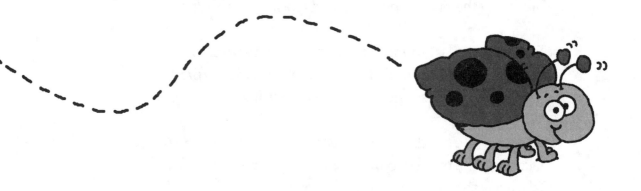

Assessment Grid

Directions: Write each child's name in the left-hand column on the grid below. Then place a check in each column that corresponds to a skill for which that child scored as competent.

A Rhyming Identification
B Rhyming Utility
C Alliteration Identification
D Alliteration Utility
E Onsets

F Rimes
G Syllabication
H Phoneme Blending
I Beginning Sounds
J Middle Sounds

K Ending Sounds
L Phoneme Counting
M Phoneme Segmentation
N Sound Deletion
O Sound Substitution

Names	A	B	C	D	E	F	G	H	I	J	K	L	M	N	O

PhoNemic AwaReness ActiVities

Stage 1: Rhyming and Alliteration Activities

1 **D**uplicate two sets of the Rhyming Picture Cards (see pp. 190–198), a set for you and a set for the children. Place 5 to 10 cards from the student set in a pile in the middle of a carpeted area. Invite children to sit around the pile. Ask one child to reach into the pile, select one card, and say the name of the item on the card. Go through your set and select another word that rhymes with the word selected by the child. Say your word aloud to the children, and then invite them to say the two rhyming words together. Repeat this activity several times. After children are comfortable with this format, increase the number of cards in the student pile to about 15 to 20 cards for successive games.

2 **S**elect several sets of the Rhyming Picture Cards. Write a sentence on the chalkboard that ends with one of the words in a rhyming set. Instead of writing the word, tape the selected picture card to the chalkboard at the end of the sentence. Read the sentence aloud to the children. Invite them to repeat it after you. Remove the picture card and tape another rhyming word from the set in its place. Read the new sentence to children and invite them to repeat it after you. Repeat this activity several times with other sets of Rhyming Picture Cards.

3 Select any six sets of Rhyming Picture Cards. Duplicate the cards, paste the duplicated cards on sheets of oaktag or construction paper, laminate them, and cut them out. Shuffle the cards and place them face down in front of a group of children. Invite one child to turn over two of the cards. If the pictures on those two cards represent two rhyming words, then the child may keep that pair of cards. If the two pictures do not rhyme, the child must return the cards to their previous locations. Another child then takes a turn with two more cards. This variation of "Concentration" can be used as a delightful review activity throughout the year.

Variation: Invite children to create their own "Concentration" cards. Invite them to cut out pictures from several old magazines and paste the pictures onto individual index cards. Flip over the cards and ask children to find matching pairs of rhyming words.

4 Select ten pairs of Rhyming Picture Cards. Provide each of ten children with an individual card. Provide a matching rhyming card to each child in another group of ten. Place each of the children in the first group in a specific location in the classroom. Tell them that they are in "nests" and that they must remain standing where they are. Tell the other group of children that they are each "birds." When you give the signal, each of the "birds" must locate her or his corresponding "nest."

Variation: After each "bird" has located her or his "nest," invite each pair to think of other words that rhyme with the two words they have. Plan opportunities for the various pairs to share their rhyming word groups.

5 Select three words from the Word Families list on pages 184–189 (two words that rhyme and one extra word). Tell children that you will say three words to them, but that only two of them rhyme or share a common sound. Invite children to identify the extra word. This can be done in a variety of ways.

- First, read several sets of rhyming pairs to children. Invite them to note how the two words in each pair are similar (they rhyme).

- After you have read a set of rhyming words to the children, invite them to repeat the pair to you. You may wish to turn this into a "sing-song" game with you and the children going back and forth.

- Place three children on chairs in the front of the room. Have the first child hold a card with the the number 1 on it, the second child hold a card with 2 on it, and the third child with 3 on it. Say the three words in random order. If the second word is the "odd" one, the second child stands up; if the third word is the "odd" one, the third child stands up; and if the first word is "odd," the first child stands up.

- Print the numbers 1, 2, and 3 on the chalkboard. Make each number about one foot high. Invite one child to come to the front of the room. Say the three words. Invite the child to stand in front of the number that represents the "odd" word. Say the words again and ask the class if the selected child is standing in front of the correct number.

6 Invite all the children to stand up. Tell them that you will be asking them a question about a rhyming word. Ask them to listen carefully, and after you have asked the question, they are to point to a designated body part (see the following chart) that rhymes with the selected word. Here's the procedure:

- Select a word from one of the four groups on the next page (for example, *see*).

- Create a question using the word (for example, "Do you know a word that rhymes with *see*?").

- Encourage students to point to the correct body part (for example, *knee*).

- Invite them to use the name of the body part in a sentence (for example, "That word is *knee*.").

- Repeat with other words.

Head	Hand	Knee	Feet
bed	sand	me	meet
dead	land	see	seat
red	stand	we	beat
led	brand	tree	greet
sled	band	free	sheet
fed	grand	tea	heat
shed	and	flea	sleet
sped			neat
wed			wheat
shred			treat

7 **S**elect six different sets of Rhyming Picture Cards (twelve cards total). Arrange the cards into a 4-x-4 square (see the samples on the next page) with the pictures randomly distributed. Photocopy one copy of the square. Rearrange the cards in a new random pattern and photocopy again. Continue rearranging the cards in several random patterns (photocopying each new pattern) until you have enough for each child in a group. Provide each child with several markers such as M&Ms®, peanuts, coins, or beans. Tell the children that you are going to play a rhyming game with them (a variation of "Tic-Tac-Toe"). You will say a word (selected from a corresponding Word Families group) and they must look on their sheets for a picture of an item that rhymes with the word you say. If there is a corresponding picture on a child's sheet, he or she can place a marker in that space. The winner is the first child to get four items in a row (horizontally, vertically, or diagonally). This is a fun game that children love to play. It can be used throughout the length of your phonemic awareness program as an active and energetic way to help children learn rhyming words.

Variation: After children are comfortable with this game, invite them to suggest a list of rhyming words that could be used to create the picture "Tic-Tac-Toe" boards. The use of student-generated words will help ensure the success of this activity.

8 Invite children as a group to select one of the Rhyming Picture Cards. Post the card at the top of a special bulletin board. Provide children with several old magazines and invite each to cut out a picture of an item that rhymes with the word posted at the top of the bulletin board. Post each selected picture on the bulletin board. Plan time (over the course of several days) to review all the rhyming words (along with the target word) with the children.

Hint: After completing the bulletin board display, take a photograph of it. Place the developed picture in a scrapbook. Add additional photographs of successive bulletin boards throughout the year. Plan time periodically to review previous bulletin board displays with the children.

9

Tell the children that you will say three words together, all of which rhyme. You want them to listen carefully and then suggest one more word for each set that rhymes with the first three words. For example, you could say *bat, cat, sat*. They might respond with *rat* or *fat* or *mat*.

The success of this activity lies in making sure that each set of three words will produce a fourth word that is within the children's listening and speaking vocabularies. It's also important that all words used are one-syllable words. Here are some possibilities:

tell, spell, fell, _____

pink, sink, link, _____

cop, top, mop, _____

pail, sail, tail, _____

fan, tan, can, _____

pill, fill, sill, _____

sip, tip, lip, _____

saw, paw, raw, _____

rice, mice, twice, _____

pin, tin, bin, _____

sit, pit, bit, _____

cap, tap, map, _____

Hints:

• The use of nonsense words to complete each line is perfectly acceptable and may even be encouraged for children with limited speaking/listening vocabularies.

• You may have children who are inclined to repeat one of the words in the set of three words as the fourth and final rhyming word. That's okay. The intent is to help children hear the rhyming patterns in words. Repeating this activity several times over a period of several days will help strengthen this important skill.

10 **U**se the following incomplete rhymes with children. Invite them to suggest a word to fill in each blank.

Note: Kids love this activity because it fosters a sense of silliness and playfulness in the classroom.

Snake, snake
Eat a _____.

Bear, bear
Eat a _____.

Cat, cat
Eat a _____.

Mouse, mouse
Eat a _____.

Dog, dog
Eat a _____.

Fly, fly
Eat a _____.

Fish, fish
Eat a _____.

Goat, goat
Eat a _____.

11 **I**nvite the children to sit in a circle. Select one of the words from a set in the Word Families section of this book. Say the word aloud to the children. Toss a ball or a beanbag to another child in the group and invite that child to think of a word that rhymes with the first word. After the child has said her or his word, she or he tosses the ball or beanbag to another child in the circle. That child also thinks of a rhyming word and then tosses the beanbag or ball to another child. The game continues until the children cannot think of any more rhyming words. The child holding the beanbag or ball at the end thinks of a new word and the game starts all over again.

12 **P**lay a game of "I Spy" with children. Begin the game by sitting with the children in a large circle. Create a sentence with two rhyming words (for example, "I spy a mat and a cat," or "I spy a tree and a knee."). Then turn to the child sitting to your right and invite that individual to create her or his own "I Spy" sentence.

Hint: Begin the game by identifying an object that is within the children's field of vision (something in the classroom)—for example, "I spy a coat and a boat," or "I spy a door and a score." (The second item does not need to be in the field of vision but should be a complimentary rhyming word.)

Variations:

• You may wish to use some Rhyming Cards as an added variation. Or, consider mixing some Rhyming Cards with visible items in the room.

• Use children's names for the "I Spy" sentences—for example, "I spy a Paul and a stall," or "I spy an Isabel and a pretty shell." (The second word can be a nonsense word—this adds a note of silliness to the game.)

13 **S**elect one of the Animal Picture Cards (see pp. 199–203) and place it in a pocket chart. Say the name of the animal for the children. Invite children to think of a word that rhymes with the name of the animal. Write the suggested word on an index card and place it in the pocket chart next to the Animal Picture Card. Tell children that you are going to use the two words in a sentence. Make up a sentence and say it for the children. Invite them to identify the two rhyming words in the sentence.

For example, you might select the Animal Picture Card for *frog*. Place that card in the pocket chart. Invite children to think of a rhyming word. They might suggest *log*. Make up a complete sentence using those two words, for example, "The frog jumped over the log." If you selected *cat*, children might suggest the word *mat*. You could create the sentence, "The cat slept on the mat."

14 Work with children in creating a variation of the song "One Potato, Two Potato." Substitute the number at the end of the third line with a word from one of the Word Family lists. Then substitute the name in the fourth line with the name of a child in the class. Place a blank at the end of the fourth line, and as you sing the song to the class, invite children to create an appropriate rhyming word for that blank. Here are three examples:

One Potato
Two Potato
Three Potato, ham.
I see Clarice eating lots of _____ .

One Potato
Two Potato
Three Potato, sled.
I see Tyrone sleeping in his _____ .

One Potato
Two Potato
Three Potato, pill.
I see Margaret sliding down a  .

15 Invite children to sit in a circle on the floor. Tell them that you are going on an imaginary "bear hunt." You will say the name of one item that you will be taking on your "bear hunt" along with another item that rhymes with the first one (you may wish to tell children that the "rules" only allow you to take rhyming objects). For example:

I'm going on a bear hunt and I'm taking a *can* and a *fan*.

Invite each child in the group to say, "I'm going on a bear hunt and I'm taking a _____ and a _____." (Substitute two rhyming words in place of the blanks.)

Hint: If children have difficulty with this activity, invite them to look around the room for an item to take on the "bear hunt." These items could include *chair, clock, pen, shoe, sack, sock,* or *floor*. After locating an item in the room, invite children to create a corresponding rhyming word.

16 Invite the children to sit in a large circle in the middle of the room. Tell them that you are going to take them on an imaginary trip. You will say the name of one item that you will take on your trip. The child sitting to your left will repeat the item and then add another item that uses a word that begins with the same sound. The activity continues until no more words can be identified. For example, you say, "I'm going deep into the jungle and I'm taking a pencil." The child on your left might say, "I'm going deep into the jungle and I'm taking a pencil and a parrot." The next child might say, "I'm going deep into the jungle and I'm taking a pencil, a parrot, and a piano."

Variation: Play the game again, but use rhyming words; for example, "I'm going deep into the jungle and I'm taking a ring, a king, a wing, and a string."

17 Work with the children to create a variation of the song "B–I–N–G–O." Sing the song for children. Then invite children to create a new name for the dog that rhymes with the first name. Continue singing the song, except that instead of eliminating letters, children insert new names each time. Each name rhymes with the previous ones. For example:

There was a farmer had a dog	There was a farmer had a dog
And Bingo was his name O.	And Tingo was his name O.
B–I–N–G–O	T–I–N–G–O
B–I–N–G–O	T–I–N–G–O
B–I–N–G–O	T–I–N–G–O
And Bingo was his name O.	And Tingo was his name O.

18 **C**ut apart the Animal Picture Cards or the Rhyming Picture Cards. Post the cards in a random arrangement on one wall of the classroom. Tell the children that you will sing a song that has a riddle in it. The children are to listen carefully to the song and then suggest a word from the posted words to be placed in the blank at the end of the fourth line. For example:

I know a word that begins with /m/,
I know a word that begins with /m/,
I know a word that begins with /m/,
And that word is _____.

(Notice that you are to make the sound of the initial phoneme at the end of the first three lines; you are not to say the name of the letter.)

Variations:

• Repeat the activity again, but this time use a word at the end of the first three lines. For example:

I know a word that rhymes with *bake*,
I know a word that rhymes with *bake*,
I know a word that rhymes with *bake*,
And that word is _____.

• Repeat the activity above using different rhyming words at the end of the first three lines. For example:

I know a word that rhymes with *bat*,
I know a word that rhymes with *cat*,
I know a word that rhymes with *fat*,
And that word is _____.

19 **A**lliterations are words that all "start the same." Introduce this concept to children by creating simple alliterative sentences that use the names of children in the room. For example:

Robert rests.
Danielle dances.
Terry taps.

Invite children (in a large group) to repeat each sentence after you. Ask them to listen for the sound at the beginning of each word in the sentence. What do they notice about the sounds at the beginning of all the words in each sentence?

After creating several two-word sentences, invent three-word sentences, each of which has the name of a child in the room. For example:

> Jacob jumps joyfully.
> Maria makes mud pies.
> Brian bounces basketballs.

Encourage children to repeat each sentence after you have said it out loud.

Afterward, create some four-word alliterative sentences, each of which contains a child's name. For example:

> Willie wears western wear.
> Bill beats big bugs.
> Sally sips salty soup.

Hint: Say each sentence slowly enough for children to hear the beginning sound in each individual word.

20 **H**ere's a great activity that will help children learn each other's names, especially at the beginning of the year. Invite each child to lay down on a large sheet of newsprint. Use a pencil to draw around the body outline of each individual. Invite parent volunteers to help you cut out the body outline of each child from the newsprint.

Provide each child with a set of crayons or colored pencils. Invite children to draw their faces on the individual body outlines. When completed, use a large marker and print each child's name on the chest area of his or her body outline. Draw a line under the first letter of the child's name.

Invite children to think of things they like (to do, to play with, to eat). Each item must begin with the same sound as their name. Print each item a child names on his or her respective body outline.

These outlines can be posted along one wall of the classroom and items can be printed on each one during the first few weeks of school. Each day select one child and recite the items on his or her outline for the entire class. ("Look, Patty likes pancakes, pickles, plants, popcorn, parties, pink, and purple.")

21 Use the name of a child to create the following verse (it can be sung in a sing-song fashion to any tune you select). The first line repeats the name of a child three times. The second line uses the name of the child along with an action verb (a word that begins with the same sound as the beginning of the student's name). The third line repeats the first, and the fourth line repeats the second. "Sing" the verse out loud for the class and then invite them to repeat it along with you. Here are two examples:

Terry, Terry, Terry
Terry talks.
Terry, Terry, Terry
Terry talks.

Ramon, Ramon, Ramon
Ramon races.
Ramon, Ramon, Ramon
Ramon races.

22 Collect an individual photograph for each child in the class. Each day select a different child and post her or his photograph on a special bulletin board. Work with children to create an adjective that also begins with the same sound as the name of the identified child. Write the child's name and the accompanying adjective underneath the photograph. Tell children that throughout the day, whenever they address or talk about that individual, they must use the adjective in combination with the child's name.

For example, "Would Tall Tony please come to the front of the room?" "Silly Sally, you can use the bathroom now," "Tumbling Tyrone has something to share with us today," or "Young Yolanda has a very pretty dress."

23 **P**rovide a group of children with an egg carton and a handful of beans. Tell the children that you will say a sentence in which each word begins with the same sound. They are to listen carefully and put a bean in a compartment for each word they hear. Create a series of alliterative sentences beginning with two-word sentences and moving up to five-word sentences. Say each sentence and invite children to place the appropriate number of beans in the compartments. For example, if you say, "Five frogs flew," children would put a bean in three adjoining compartments in the egg carton. If you said, "Larry Light laughed loud," children would place a bean in four adjoining compartments. Create a series of various alliterative sentences to share with the children.

Hint: Whenever possible, use the names of children in creating the alliterative sentences.

24 **A**s you share a book with children, invite them to note the names of characters in the story. After you have completed reading the story, write the names of the major characters on the chalkboard. Read the names for the children as you point to them. Then, invite the children to participate in one of the following activities:

• Ask children to think of words that have the same beginning letter as the name of the character. Add that word to the character's name and say it for children. Invite them to repeat the phrase to you—for example, "Animal Arthur," "Penny Popcorn," or "Tall Teddy."

• Ask children to think of words that rhyme with the name of a book character. After children have identified a rhyming word for a character, invite them to say the name of the character. Respond with the rhyming word. You and the children can go back and forth with this several times. For example, *sheep* and *sleep*. Children say *sheep*, you respond with *sleep*. Repeat three times.

25 Use several old magazines and cut out four or five examples of pictures which all begin with the same sound. Glue each of the pictures onto a 4-x-6-inch index card. Create six or seven sets of these cards. Mix up the cards. String a length of twine or yarn across the front of the classroom and place several clothespins along the yarn.

Select one of the cards and show it to the children. Say the name of the item in the picture and invite children to listen carefully for the beginning sound. Clip the card with a clothespin to one end of the yarn. Invite one child to select another card from the stack and give it to you. Say the name of the item on the card and invite children to tell you if it has the same beginning sound as the first item. If they agree that it does, clip it to the yarn next to the target word. If the card does not represent the target sound, put it in a separate pile. After all the cards for a single sound have been clipped to the yarn, say all the words and invite children to repeat the entire list back to you. Remove all the cards from the yarn and repeat the activity with another target sound.

Hint: As children become proficient with this activity, invite them to cut pictures from old magazines and paste them on 4-x-6-inch index cards. Work with children in a large-group sorting activity, dividing the large pile into several select piles, with each picture in a pile representing a single initial sound.

26 **C**hildren can create silly alliterative sentences with the following activity. Place one of the Animal Picture Cards in a pocket chart. Say the name of the animal for children. Demonstrate to children how the word for that picture can be used in a silly sentence, a sentence in which every word begins with the same sound. For example, if you place a picture of a fish in the chart, you might create the following sentence: "Five fish finally flew." Or if you put the picture of a bat in the pocket chart, you might create the following sentence, "Big bad bats bugged Boston."

Variations:

- Invite individual children to select a random Animal Picture Card and place it in the pocket chart. They can then challenge you to create a silly sentence.

- After children are comfortable, invite them to create a silly sentence using a random Animal Picture Card.

- Place an Animal Picture Card in the pocket chart. Create a two-word alliterative sentence. Invite children to repeat it after you. Then, using the same card, create a three-word alliterative sentence. Invite children to repeat it. Using the same card once again, create a four-word alliterative sentence and invite children to repeat it. For example, for *cow*:

> Cows cut.
> Crazy cows cut.
> Crazy cows cut cartoons.

Stage 2:
Word Parts Activities

1 **U**se the song "Old MacDonald Had a Farm" to help children learn about onsets and rimes. Select a word from the Word Families list. Write it on a large index card and post it on a bulletin board or chalkboard. Tell children you are going to show them how this word can be separated into two different parts. Insert the onset, rime, and complete word into the song and sing it for children. Afterward, invite children to sing along with you as you repeat the song. Here are two examples:

Sing

Old Macdonald had a *sing*
E–I–E–I–O
With an /s/ /s/ here
And an /ing/ /ing/ there
Here an /s/
There an /ing/
Everywhere a /sing/ /sing/
Old Macdonald had a sing
E–I–E–I–O.

Pill

Old Macdonald had a *pill*
E–I–E–I–O
With a /p/ /p/ here
And a /ill/ /ill/ there
Here a /p/
There an /ill/
Everywhere a /pill/ /pill/
Old Macdonald had a pill
E–I–E–I–O.

2 Invite the children to sit in a circle on the floor. Tell them that you will say the name of a child in the room. Demonstrate how to clap the child's name according to the number of syllables in the name (for example, Hector—two claps, Annabelle—three claps). Go through your class list and say the name of each child. Invite the entire class to clap each child's name.

Variations:

• Say the name of a child who has a one-syllable name. Invite all the other children who have one-syllable names to clap once (at the same time). Say the name of a child with a two-syllable name and invite all the other children with two-syllable names to clap twice at the same time. Repeat with three-syllable names, four-syllable names, and so on.

• Secretly select the name of a child in your class. Clap that child's name. Invite all the children whose names have the same number of syllables as the identified child to stand up and say their names. Invite children to notice that all the names have something in common. Repeat with other names.

3 Bring in an old lunchbox (easily obtained at a garage or yard sale). Cover it with colored sticky-backed drawer liner paper and decorate it to look like a treasure chest. Place several objects in the treasure chest, each of which has a two-syllable name. If necessary, you may wish to select photographs or illustrations from old magazines, cut them out, and paste them onto sheets of oaktag or construction paper.

Invite one child to reach into the treasure chest and select an object (such as a pencil, notebook, crayon, or thumbtack). Invite the child to name the object selected. Show children how the name of the object actually comprises two parts or two syllables. Invite children to clap the syllables so that everyone is involved. Invite other children to reach into the treasure chest to select and identify other two-syllable items.

Variation: Create several different treasure chests—for example, a three-syllable treasure chest and/or a four-syllable treasure chest. If necessary, you may wish to begin with a one-syllable treasure chest.

Hint: After children are familiar with the types of items that belong in each specific treasure chest, invite them to contribute items for one or more of the treasure chests. These can be actual items or pictures cut from old magazines. You may then wish to begin each day with a "Treasure Chest Hunt."

4 **U**se strips of masking tape to create a series of three boxes on the floor of the classroom. Make each box approximately 2 feet x 2 feet. Use additional strips of masking tape to create a number inside each of the boxes. One box will have a 1, another box will have a 2, and the third box will have a 3 taped to the inside.

Select several one-, two-, and three-syllable words from a book you are sharing with children. Invite the children to stand in a line behind the boxes. Tell them that you will say a word. They should listen very carefully and decide how many parts (syllables) are in the word you say. Then, one at a time, they should move forward and stand in the box whose number indicates the number of syllables in the selected word. Afterward, each child can return to the back of the line. Continue until every child has gone through the line twice.

Variations:

• Invite other children to agree or disagree with the choice using a thumbs-up or thumbs-down motion.

• Place children in pairs. Say a word and invite a pair of children to talk with each other and decide on the number of syllables in the selected word. One of the two children can then move forward and stand in the appropriate box on the floor.

Note: This is a good activity for children learning English.

5 Select several words from the Animal Picture cards (two-syllable words) on pages 202–203. Say each word to the children and invite them to repeat each word after you say it. Then, select one of the words and tell the children that you are going to separate it into two parts. Say the first syllable of the word. Then, using your arms or hands, make an imaginary motion, such as making a karate chop, sawing a board in two, swinging an ax, or another appropriate "separation motion." Afterward, say the second syllable of the word. Repeat this with three or four other words.

Select additional words and invite children to follow along with you as you say the first syllable, chop through the air with a hand, and then say the second syllable. Explain to children that the "karate chop" is a way of separating selected words into two different parts.

Variation:

- Write several of the words on large 5-x-8-inch index cards. Use a pair of scissors to cut each word into its two syllables. Show the cards to the children. Say the first syllable and ask children to repeat after you. Pretend to tear or rip the two parts of the card apart. Then, say the second syllable and invite children to repeat after you.

- Repeat as above, but this time invite a child to stand near you and assist in "tearing" the two parts of the card away from each other. Invite other children to engage in this physical "separation" of a word into two individual syllables. As children become more adept at syllabication, invite them to do this with three- and four-syllable words.

6 Select several words from the Word Families lists on pages 184–189. Tell children that you are going to say these words to them, but that you are going to do something special with each word. Loop a long rubber band around the index finger of your left hand and the index finger of your right hand. Hold the rubber band in front of your mouth. Say a selected word to the children very slowly while at the same time stretching the rubber band in front of your mouth. Repeat with other words from the Word Families lists.

Afterward, invite students to do the same thing, except that they will be using *imaginary* rubber bands. Ask each child to hold his or her index fingers next to his or her mouth as though the fingers had a rubber band between them. Invite children to repeat a word you select, saying it very slowly and pulling the fingers apart as he or she says the word (be sure to model this action with your own rubber band). Tell children that they are "rubber banding" their words, stretching out the sounds in a single word.

Hint: Periodically throughout the day, invite selected children to "rubber band" a word that they have just said. This can be a random activity, done occasionally within the context of other activities. Keep the emphasis on fun and informality, and this activity may develop into a longtime favorite of children.

7 **H**ere's a fun and easy way to help children practice and understand the nature of blending sounds together. Tell the children that when you read a book or story to them, you will s-t-r-e-t-c-h out selected words. Each time you stretch a word, stop and invite children to say the word that you have stretched.

You may wish to alert children ahead of time that you are about to say a stretched word. For example, just before you begin to say a stretched word, put your finger on your nose or tap the top of your head three times.

Here's an example from the book *Slugs* by Anthony D. Fredericks (Minneapolis, MN: Lerner Publications, 2000):

> If slugs go out in the s–u–n, they will dry up. Slugs hide f–r–o–m the sun in moist soil. They also hide under plants or under r–o–ck–s.

Hint: Select words with which the students are familiar or that are within their listening vocabularies. Also, don't stretch more than three words per paragraph. Doing so will seriously detract from their enjoyment of the story. You may wish to consider doing this activity on the third or fourth reading of a book.

8 **T**ell children that you will talk to them as a ghost would, stretching out words. When you say a "ghost word," encourage children to tell you what the word is—for example, "I went into the haunted hhhooooooowwwwwssssss," or "There was a black cccccccaaaaaaaattttttt in the yard."

After children are comfortable with ghost words, invite them to create their own ghost words to say to each other. Tell the children that they can only include one ghost word in each sentence. Encourage individual children to say a sentence with a ghost word in it and invite the remainder of the class to say what the word was.

Hint: This is one of my favorite activities. I usually preface each ghost word with a frightened or scared expression on my face as a clue to children that a ghost word is about to be said.

9 **T**ell children that you are going to teach them a variation of "Row, Row, Row Your Boat" using their names. Sing the following song and insert the name of one child at the end. As you say the name of the child, divide it into individual phonemes, and ask the entire class to blend those phonemes together to create the name of a specific individual in the class. You may wish to pre-select a child and invite her or him to stand next to you as you sing the song with the children:

Say, say, say the sounds
Gently in a row
Slowly, slowly, slowly
This is how they go.
    You say: /A/ /l/ /a/ /n/ /a/
    Children say: Alana

Say, say, say the sounds
Gently in a row
Slowly, slowly, slowly
This is how they go.
> You say: /P/ /e/ /t/ /er/
> Children say: Peter

Variations:

- Invite children to sing the song; you say the phonemes and the child's name.

- Invite children to sing the song; you say the phonemes and they say the child's name.

- You sing the song and say the phonemes; children say the child's name.

10 Invite children to tell you the names of animals. As they say the names, write them on the chalkboard or a sheet of newsprint fastened to the wall. After you have obtained a sufficient number of animals (20 or more), tell the children that you are going to ask them some riddles (make sure that children understand that a riddle is nothing more than a fun question along with a clue to the answer of that question). Let the children know that the riddles you ask will involve the animal names you have written down. Here are some examples:

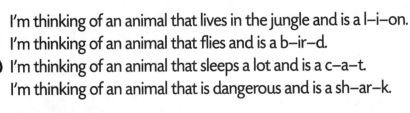

I'm thinking of an animal that lives in the jungle and is a l–i–on.
I'm thinking of an animal that flies and is a b–ir–d.
I'm thinking of an animal that sleeps a lot and is a c–a–t.
I'm thinking of an animal that is dangerous and is a sh–ar–k.

Variations:

- You may wish to initiate this activity through the use of the Animal Picture Cards. Later, you can combine the Animal Picture Cards with names of animals suggested by the children.

- As students become familiar with this activity, you may wish to focus on animal words within a selected category—for example, "Farm Animals," "Ocean Animals," or "Desert Animals."

11 With a roll of masking tape, create a rectangle on the floor of the classroom (preferably in the front of the room). Tape pieces of masking tape to the floor in a 2-x-6-foot rectangle. Tell the children that this rectangle is the Slow-Down Box. That means that any time someone is in this box, they must say a word very, very slowly. Demonstrate this for children by walking across the front of the room saying a few words with which children are familiar. When you get inside the Slow-Down Box, say the next word very slowly, stretching out the individual sounds in the word. Continue walking through the box and out the other end.

Now, invite a child to walk across the front of the room, duplicating what you did. Provide a word for the child selected from the children's speaking vocabularies (or she or he can repeat the same words you used). When the child gets within the boundaries of the Slow-Down Box, remind her or him to say the next word v-e-r-y s-l-o-w-l-y. Invite other children to repeat this activity.

Hints:

- Children enjoy this activity enormously, particularly when the Box is left on the floor for the duration of the day. Then, any time someone walks across the room and through the box, she or he must say a word very slowly. Alert any visitors ahead of time and invite them to walk through the Slow-Down Box saying a word very slowly.
- After each "walk-through" in the Slow-Down Box, invite children to say the target word in its normal way. Ensure that children understand the relationship between the "stretched" word and its normal usage.

12 After you have read a book or story to the children, select several different words. Print each word on a 5-x-8-inch index card. Use a pair of scissors to cut apart the cards, phoneme by phoneme, in a zigzag pattern to create two or more puzzle pieces. Place the pieces from one word into a small manila envelope. Glue a picture, illustration, or drawing of the object named on the card on the outside of the envelope (this will serve as an important clue for children). Repeat for other words.

Provide individual children (or pairs of children) with a selected envelope. Invite children to assemble the pieces in the envelope to create a word. Tell them that an illustration of the word is pasted on the outside of the envelope. Let children know that when they have each assembled their puzzles pieces into a word, you will come over and say the word for them.

Tell children that each puzzle piece for a selected word represents a sound within that word. When they put the pieces together, they are also putting the sounds of the word together. When the sounds go together, then you (the teacher) are able to say a complete word.

Hint: You may wish to reread the selected piece of literature, emphasizing the words that were identified for this activity.

13 **P**lace three chairs in the front of the room. Invite three children to each select a chair and sit down. Give each child a number, starting with 1. Tell the three children that you will say three different words, one for each number. The sound at the beginning of two of those words will be the same. The other word will be different. Invite two of the children to stand up if their sounds are the same. For example, if you said *dog*, *dare*, and *song*, then children 1 and 2 would stand up. If you said *cat*, *wing*, and *cost*, then children 1 and 3 would stand up. If you said *bun*, *tub*, and *top*, then children 2 and 3 would stand up.

Select the words from the Word Families lists. You may also wish to use words from a book that you are sharing with the children as part of a read-aloud activity.

Variation: Repeat this activity using three words, two of which have the same ending sound and one of which does not.

14 **T**each the children a new version of the song, "If You're Happy and You Know It." At the end of the song, say a word from a recently read book or story. Say the word in parts, and invite the children to put the parts (phonemes) together to form a word. Sing the song several times, each time using a different word from the story.

> If you hear all the sounds, make them whole.
> If you hear all the sounds, make them whole.
> If you hear all the sounds,
> If you hear all the sounds,
> If you hear all the sounds, make them whole.
>   (/s/ /a/ /t/)

Variations:

- Select action verbs from the story. After children have identified a selected word and blended the sounds together, encourage them to perform the action, either individually or collectively. For example, the word is *sat*. After blending the phonemes together and saying the word, ask all the children to sit down.

- Invite children to contribute potential words for this activity. Encourage them to think of words they have heard in a story, words heard at home, or even their own favorite words. Include one or more of these words in future renditions of the song.

15

Invite children to stand in a circle. Sing the following song to the class and invite each designated child to say the name of the person standing to her or his right very slowly (children may wish to "rubber band" the names). Then all children stamp their feet and says the designated child's name correctly. Here are three examples:

Jonathan, Jonathan
How do you do?
Who's that person next to you?
>Jonathan says, "/C/ . . . /ar/ . . . /m/ . . . /e/ . . . /l/ . . . /a/."
>The class collectively stomps their feet and says, "Carmella."

Carmella, Carmella
How do you do?
Who's that person next to you?
>Carmella says, "/B/ . . . /r/ . . . /e/ . . . /n/ . . . /d/ . . . /a/."
>The class collectively stomps their feet and says, "Brenda."

Brenda, Brenda
How do you do?
Who's that person next to you?
>Brenda says, "/S/ . . . /a/ . . . /b/ . . . /i/ . . . /n/."
>The class collectively stomps their feet and says, "Sabine."

Stage 3: Sound Positions Activities

1 **T**each the children the following verse. This verse can be sung in a military-type cadence (similar to the ditties soldiers sing back and forth when marching).

Students:	There's a sound that's in my ear.
You:	What's the *first* sound you can hear?
Students:	Tell us some words–one, two, three.
You:	Then you must listen carefully: *bake, bail, bank*
Students:	/b/

Students:	There's a sound that's in my ear.
You:	What's the *first* sound you can hear?
Students:	Tell us some words–one, two, three.
You:	Then you must listen carefully: *girl, goose, get*
Students:	/g/

Repeat the song several times, each time selecting a trio of words (from the Word Families lists on pages 184–189) with the same beginning sound.

Variation: The song can be altered slightly to focus on the *"last* sound you can hear?"

2 **S**elect a target sound for the day (for example, /b/). Invite children to look through old magazines for pictures or illustrations of objects that each begins with the target sound (for example, *boy, basket, ball, bone*). Encourage the children to paste all their pictures onto a large sheet of oaktag or construction paper to create an oversize collage.

After a "Daily Collage" has been created, take time during the day to have the children say all of the represented words on the collage. Invite children to note how all the words begin with the same sound. Plan time for students to create a collage a day, each one focusing on words that all begin with the same sound.

Variation: After children have become familiar with the above activity, invite them to create "Daily Collages," each of which focuses on a single sound at the end of selected words. Please note that this variation is a challenging activity for most children.

3 **A**n alternate method of introducing initial sounds to children involves a slight modification of the activity above. Gather together several large manila envelopes. Collect several old magazines. Identify and cut out pictures, each of which begins with an identical sounds (for example, pictures of objects that all begin with /b/, objects that all begin with /m/, objects that all begin with /l/).

Paste each picture on a 3-x-5-inch index card. Put all the pictures with the same beginning sound in the same envelope. Prepare several separate envelopes.

Arrange the children into several small groups. Provide each group with an envelope. Instruct the children to remove all the picture cards from the envelope and identify the objects on each one. Invite each group to tell you the beginning sound for all the items in the envelope. Afterward, ask each group to replace the cards into their envelope. Redistribute the envelopes among the groups and repeat the activity.

Variation: Remove a few cards from each envelope and invite the children to sort the pictures by beginning sounds.

4 **O**btain an extra copy of each child's school photograph. Invite each child to glue her or his photo to the end of a craft stick. Place the children on the floor in a large circle. Call on one child to say a familiar word (for example, *dog*). Afterward, call out another word (which may or may not have the same beginning sound; for example, *dump*). If the word you call out has the same beginning sound, the children are all to hold their "picture sticks" in the air. If the word you say does not have the same beginning sound, then the picture sticks are to stay on the floor.

Go around the circle once or twice, ensuring that each child has one or two opportunities to say a word (followed by a word that you select).

Note: If all the children respond to each question, you will be able to note who isn't "getting it." This will allow you to form small groups for specialized instruction.

Variation: Repeat this circle game with the focus on words that may or may not have the same ending sounds.

5 **P**lay a variation of "Simon Says" with the children. Select several words from the Word Families lists. Tell the children that you will ask them a question that they must answer with a "Yes" or a "No," but only if "Simon Says."

Line up the children in a straight line. Tell them that if they answer correctly (and only when "Simon Says"), then they get to step forward one step. If they answer incorrectly or answer correctly (but not when "Simon Says"), then they must remain where they are. Here are some sample questions:

Beginning Sounds

- Simon says the following words all have the same beginning sound: *pan, pick, pill.*

- Simon says the following words all have the same beginning sound: *sub, sink, fog.*

- The following words all have the same beginning sound: *sap, sing, sun.*

Middle Sounds

- Simon says the following words all have the same middle sound: *cub, fun, cut.*

- Simon says the following words all have the same middle sound: *rot, hum, hot.*

- The following words all have the same middle sound: *gate, rake, pail.*

Ending Sounds

- Simon says the following words all have the same ending sound: *map, chip, peep.*

- Simon says the following words all have the same ending sound: *coat, mad, rid.*

- The following words all have the same ending sound: *jack, lake, brick.*

6 **O**btain several old work gloves (these can often be found at yard sales, Goodwill Industries, or Salvation Army stores, or can be donated by friends and neighbors). Cut off all the fingers from the gloves. Purchase some fabric paint at a local craft, hobby, or variety store. Paint one-half of the "fingers" red and the other half of the "fingers" green.

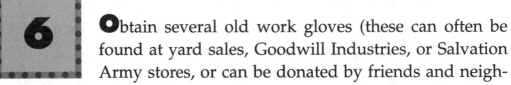

After the "fingers" are dry, provide each child with one green "finger" and one red "finger." Instruct children to put the red "finger" on a finger of one hand and the green "finger" on a finger on the other hand (some assistance may be necessary).

Select a target sound (/s/, for example). Tell the children to hold up a green (for "go") finger every time they hear the target sound at the beginning of a word. Tell them to hold up a red finger (for "stop") if they do not hear the target sound at the beginning of a word.

Read selected words from a children's book. Encourage children to indicate which ones have the target sound at the beginning. Periodically, select a new target sound and a new set of words.

Variations:

- Repeat this activity with a familiar song, poem, finger play, or nursery rhyme.

- This activity works equally well with a target sound at the ends of words.

7 **D**raw three vertical lines (top to bottom) on the classroom chalkboard, separating it into three equal sections. Draw an illustration of a snake on a transparency master (a sheet of acetate). Use an overhead projector to project the snake onto the chalkboard (the effect will be that the three vertical lines on the chalkboard will divide the snake into three sections). Place a very large X on a 5-x-8-inch index card. Glue a small magnet to the back of the card (if you have a magnetic board) or place a doughnut of masking tape on the back of the card.

Say a target sound (such as /t/). Select several three-phoneme words from the Word Families lists or a current piece of children's literature being shared with the class. Say a word and invite one child to take the X card and place it in the beginning, middle, or ending section of the snake to indicate whether the sound was at the beginning, middle, or end of the word. Repeat with additional sounds and words.

Variations:

• Each child could have a "snake" and use markers to indicate whether she or he understands the positions of selected sounds.

• Instead of using an index card with an X on it, draw an illustration of a mouse on the card. After you've identified the target sound and said a three-phoneme word, invite a child to place the "mouse" card inside the snake's body (for example, the mouse is at the beginning of the snake's body, the middle, or has been completely swallowed to the end of the snake).

• If an overhead projector is not available, draw the illustration of the snake directly on the chalkboard.

• Depending on your level of artistic talent (or that of of the school's art teacher, whom you might "employ"), you can draw an illustration of yourself (in a prone position) on the chalkboard or overhead transparency master (along with the three vertical lines). Children love this variation, particularly when they get to put a "mouse" somewhere "inside" *your* "body."

8 Arrange the children in a circle. Tell them that you have a ship that is being loaded with all sorts of items. What makes this ship unusual is that it can only accept items whose names all begin with the same sound.

Identify a target sound. Begin the game by saying, "I have a ship. The ship is being loaded with cars." Turn to the child sitting to your left and invite her or him to add to your sentence. For example, "I have a ship. The ship is being loaded with cars and candy." The child then turns to the next person in the circle and invites her or him to add one more item. For example, "I have a ship. The ship is being loaded with cars, candy, and cake." The game continues until someone cannot "load" an item on the ship. At that point you can identify a new target sound and the "ship loading" procedure can begin anew.

9 Invite children to cut pictures from several old magazines. Work with them to glue individual pictures on separate 5-x-8-inch index cards. Tie several lengths of yarn (each approximately 3 feet long) from the ceiling or from light fixtures (many classrooms have drop ceilings which makes this quite easy to do).

Identify a target beginning sound (/b/, for example). Show children the picture cards, one at a time, and ask them if they hear the target sound at the beginning of the pictured word. If they do, clip the card to one length of yarn with a clothespin. If they don't hear the target sound at the beginning of a word, return the card to the pile. Go through all the cards in this manner. Repeat the process with another target sound (/k/, for example). Clip all the picture words with that beginning target sound to the same length of yarn. Periodically review the categories of beginning sounds.

Variation: This activity works equally well with middle and ending sounds. In addition, it adds a decorative and colorful touch to the classroom.

10 Duplicate, laminate, and cut out all the Animal Picture Cards. Shuffle the cards thoroughly. Invite the children to come to the front of the room one at a time and select one of the cards. Invite a child to say the name of the animal pictured on a card. Then ask each child one or more of the following questions:

What sound do you hear at the beginning of that animal's name?
What sound do you hear in the middle of that animal's name?
What sound do you hear at the end of that animal's name?

Hint: Be sure the children can do *beginning*, then *ending*, then *middle* sounds before asking for all three.

Variation: Invite youngsters to cut out pictures of animals from old magazines. Glue each picture on a 3-x-5-inch index card. Shuffle the cards and repeat the activity above.

11 Obtain several brown lunch bags. On the bottom of each bag, glue a picture of a familiar object. Turn over a bag and place it on your hand to create a puppet (the bottom of the bag becomes the top of the puppet's head). Draw an illustration of a face on the front of the bag. (By arranging your hand inside the bag, you can make the puppet have a "mouth" and "talk.")

After creating several of these (each with a different picture on top), distribute them to small groups of children, one puppet per group. Tell each group that the item pictured on the top of the puppet's head indicates what kinds of things the puppet can "eat." A puppet can only eat things that begin with the same sound as the picture on its head. For example, if there is a picture of a car on the top of a puppet's head, it can only eat cards, coins, cups, and crayons.

Invite each group to search through the room for items that begin with the same sound as indicated by the picture on the puppet's head. Give the groups five minutes to collect as many items as they can. When the time limit has expired, invite all of the groups to arrange their items on a table. Encourage each group to name all the items and note how they all begin with the same sound.

Hint: You may wish to "stack the deck" by bringing in several items from home to distribute around the classroom and add to those that would normally be found in the room.

Variation: Invite selected children to take a puppet home. Encourage them to look around the house for items that the puppet would "eat." Ask each child to bring in the identified items (with parental permission) to share with the class. Distribute the puppets to other children on successive days to continue this activity over several days.

12 Obtain several old magazines. Cut out a variety of about 40 or 50 pictures from the magazines and paste each one on a 5-x-8-inch index card. Punch holes and string yarn through each one to make a necklace. Randomly distribute the cards to the class and ask each child to name the item on her or his card. After each child has named the item, invite each child to wear her or his necklace. Now ask children to "travel" around the room locating other individuals who have an item that begins with the same sound as the item on their cards. Invite all the children with the same beginning sound to gather together in one spot in the classroom. Call on a group and invite them to say which sound brought them together and to say all of their picture words.

Continue the game by collecting all the cards, mixing them up, and redistributing them to every child. This activity can include several different "rounds."

Hint: After children have assembled in groups, ask which group had the most number of individuals and which group had the least number of individuals. If appropriate, you may wish to chart or graph these results on the chalkboard.

Variation: Invite children to focus on the ending sounds of the pictured items.

13 **O**btain three 5-x-8-inch index cards. Using a black marker, write the following words on the index cards, one to a card: FIRST, MIDDLE, and END. Punch two holes in the top of each card and thread a piece of yarn through the holes. Tie off the yarn so that a large loop is formed. Invite three children to stand in the front of the room. Place a card over the head of each of the children and stand them in order, FIRST, MIDDLE, and END.

Select a series of words from the Word Families lists. Tell the three children that you will say one of the words and ask them about certain sounds in each word. For example, the target word is *boat*:

Karen (who has the FIRST card around her neck), what was the first sound you heard in the word *boat*?

Angel (who has the MIDDLE card around her neck), what was the middle sound you heard in the word *boat*?

Kenny (who has the END card around his neck), what was the end sound you heard in the word *boat*?

Hint: Be careful how you select the children for this activity. Make sure that the selected children are comfortable with positional words.

Variation: Divide the class into three equal groups of children. Arrange the children in three lines. On each of three separate desks, place one of the cards as described above. Invite children in the first lines to step up, one at a time, to the FIRST desk; those in the second line to step up to the MIDDLE desk; and those in the third line to step up to the END desk. Say a target word and invite each of the three children at the desks to identify the first, middle, and ending sounds. If a child identifies the appropriate sound correctly, she or he gets a point for his or her team. The first team to reach 10 points (or 20 points) is the winner.

14 **I**nvite children to play a variation of "Go Fish." On each of several 3-x-5-inch index cards, glue a picture cut from an old magazine. You may wish to include some of the Animal Picture Cards as well. Make up several sets of these cards—about 25 to 30 picture cards per set. Invite each child to select a partner. Provide each pair with a "deck" of cards.

Begin the game by asking each child to select five random cards from the deck. Each child holds her or his cards so that the other person cannot see them. One child goes first and says the name of the object pictured on a card. If the other child has a card with a picture of an item that begins with that same sound, then the second child gives that card to the first child, who sets aside that pair of cards. The first child gets another turn. If the second child does not have a card with a picture that has the same beginning sound, then she or he says, "Go Fish." The first child selects a card from the deck. It's now the second child's opportunity to ask for a matching beginning sound. The game ends when all the cards have been used or one child has no more cards in her or his hand. The child with the most pairs is the winner.

Hint: I have found it advantageous to model this game first before having the children attempt it independently. I call a child to a table in the front of the room and we "play" the game in front of the rest of the class, identifying all the cards in our hands so that the "audience" can see how the game progresses.

15 Obtain an old suitcase or knapsack. Collect a variety of small objects (approximately 30 to 40) that can be paired together by beginning sounds (for example, sock + soap, cap + cup, pin + penny, dime + dollar). Lay all the items on a table and invite the children to gather around the table.

Tell the children that you are going on a trip, but that you are only allowed to take pairs of items. The name of each item in a pair must begin with the same sound. Invite children to assist you in selecting the appropriate pairs. Go around the table and ask each child to name two items with the same beginning sound. If a correct "pairing" has been made, invite that child to place the two items in the suitcase or knapsack.

Hint: Later, this activity can be used as a good learning center activity.

Variations:

- Invite children to identify three items, each with the same initial sound, to be placed into the suitcase.

- Invite the children to collect pairs of items to be placed into the suitcase. The names of each item in a pair must *end* with the same sound.

- Invite children to select items that can be found only in the classroom to be placed on the table (for example, paper clip + pencil, tack + tape, book + bag). Or, as part of a weekly "Show and Tell" experience, invite children to each bring in one secret item from home that can be added to the "collection" and placed on the table.

16 Invite children to help you create personal tongue twisters—each of which uses a child's name along with other words. All of the tongue twisters begin with the same sound. Here are some examples:

Tapping Tommy turns tables.
Happy José helps Harry.
Danny's dad delivers doughnuts.
Mary's mother makes marshmallows.
Carol keeps creepy creatures.
Richard raises red roses.

For additional reinforcement, you may wish to record these sentences on strips of newsprint and post them around the room.

Stage 4: Sound Separation Activities

1 **P**rovide each child with a paper cup. Place ten edible items, such as raisins, small candies, or peanut halves, into each cup. (Be aware of any food allergies.) Be sure to have a cup for yourself.

Tell children that you are going to count words by taking a counter out of the cup and putting it on your table for each word you say in a sentence. Explain that you will say a sentence in the normal way and then say it again, pausing after each word to take a counter out of your cup and place it on the table.

Demonstrate with the following:

Say: I run.
Say: I (Take a counter out of your cup and place it on the table.) run.
(Take a counter out of your cup and place it on the table.)

Invite the children to copy your actions as you repeat the previous sentence.

Now say a three-word sentence and repeat the sequence above. Follow with a four-word sentence and a five-word sentence, each time modeling the sentence and then inviting students to copy your actions with the identical sentences.

Note: After children have completed this activity, they can trade them in for "fresh" markers.

2 **A**fter children are comfortable with the previous activity, create original sentences, each of which includes the name of a child in the class. Start with sentences that are relatively short ("Maria laughs."). After you say the sentence, invite the children to repeat it after you. Say the sentence again, this time encouraging children to place a counter on their table for each word they hear in the sentence.

Hint: They should be placed left to right, if possible.

Do two or three two-word sentences, each with a child's name embedded in the sentence. Then progressively make the sentences longer, one word at a time. Again, include a child's name in each sentence. For example:

Cindy runs. (two words, two counters)
Harold is sick. (three words, three counters)
Michael lives next door. (four words, four counters)
April has a new bike. (five words, five counters)

Depending on the ability level(s) of children in your classroom, you should use sentences of no more than five words each.

Variations:

• After you say several five-word sentences, create sentences with progressively fewer words in them (four words, three words, and so on). End with two-word sentences.

• Provide each child with different-colored coated candy pieces. Tell them that whenever they hear the name of a person in the class, they should put down a red (or green or blue) coated candy pieces. They can use any other colors for other words in a sentence.

• As a variation on the variation above, invite children to place a green marker at the beginning of the sentence and a red marker at the end of the sentence.

3 **A**fter children know their ordinal numbers (1, 2, 3), invite them to participate in the following activity. Count out a stack of 5-x-8-inch index cards, one for each child in the class. Divide the deck into three piles. Using a large marker, put the number 2 on all the cards in one pile; 3 on all the cards in the second pile; and 4 on all the cards in the third pile. Randomly distribute all the cards to children in the class.

Tell the children that you will say a word. Invite them to listen carefully and to count the number of sounds they hear in that target word. All the children who have a number card that represents the number of sounds in the target word are to hold their cards up. For example, you say the word *bill*. All the children with a 3 card will raise their cards in the air. You say the word *on*. All the children with a number 2 card will raise their cards in the air. You can select words from the Word Families lists or from a current piece of children's literature.

Hint: Be sure to say the words slowly so students will be able to hear and differentiate the individual sounds within the target words.

4 **O**btain several old magazines. Read through the magazines and cut out photographs or illustrations of various objects. The objects you select should have two, three, or four phonemes in their names. Paste each separate object on a large index card. Divide a large sheet of newsprint or construction paper into three columns. Post this chart in the front of the room.

Shuffle all the "object cards" and place them in a large brown paper bag. Invite a child to reach into the bag and select a card at random. Encourage the child to say the name of the object on the card and to count the number of phonemes she or he hears in the object's name. Provide the child with a small piece of masking tape. Instruct the child to tape the card onto the chart in its correct category. Continue this activity with other children and other cards. For example:

After the children have posted all the cards in the deck onto the chart, review the cards, their individual phonemes, and the correct placement of each card into its proper category.

Hint: You may wish to begin by using words from the Word Families list. Later as children become more practiced, select words from a current piece of literature you are reading to the class. Then, invite the children to suggest their own words—words that can be illustrated and words that have two, three, or four phonemes. The game can be played as directed above.

5 Teach children to sing "Happy Birthday" in a new way: Each time you and the children sing the song, select a new target word for the last word in the third line. These target words can be selected from a nursery rhyme, a children's book, the Animal Picture Cards, or other word lists in this book. Then replace the last line in the song with the following line: "What's the first sound in you?"

Variation: Use a target word as the last word in line 3. Replace the last line in the song with the following: "What's the last sound in you?"

6 Obtain three wooden clothespins. Using a black marker, write the number 1 on one clothespin, the number 2 on another, and the number 3 on the last.

Select several three-letter/three-phoneme words (see the table on the next page). Write each word on a large index card in block letters. Select one card and show it to the children while saying the word aloud. Repeat the word slowly and clip an appropriately numbered clothespin to the top of the card over each phoneme/letter. Clip the 1 clothespin to the top of the card over the first phoneme; the 2 clothespin to the top of the card over the middle phoneme; and the 3 clothespin to the top of the card over the ending phoneme.

This activity visually reinforces the location and placement of individual sounds in a word.

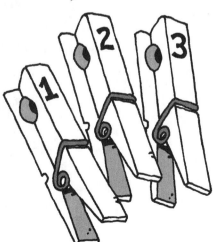

Here are a few three-letter/three-phoneme words to get you started:

bat	cup	pin
dad	bag	rag
ham	cap	cat
bed	hen	jet
pig	dog	cot

Variation: As students become familiar with this activity move them into three-phoneme/four-letter words. Then, move into four-phoneme/four-letter and four-phoneme/five-letter words.

Hint: Once you move from pictures to words, you must select the target words carefully, since silent letters or unusual sound/letter representations may confuse some children (For example: ph = /f/ in phone; gh = /f/ in cough).

7 Just for fun, tell children that you are going to play a game with each of their names. Instead of saying each child's name in its normal manner, address each child by extending and expanding the first sound in her or his name. For example:

> S-s-s-s-s-s-arah will be our lunch counter today.
> Will you please take this note to the office, M-m-m-m-m-m-iguel?
> I really like the way A-a-a-a-a-a-a-ndrew is sitting in his chair.

Hint: You may be able to use this activity with the ending sounds of some of the children's names. For example: "Did everyone see what Mark-k-k-k-k-k-k brought in today?" or "Dillon-n-n-n-n-n-n, will you please post your picture on the bulletin board?"

Variation: Use this activity when talking about other individuals in the school, such as the secretary, the principal, the librarian, the nurse, the custodian, etc.

8 Create 20 picture cards using words from the Word Families list, Animal Picture Cards list, or Rhyming Picture Cards (see pages 190–198). You may wish to select words from a current children's book you are sharing with the class or a familiar nursery rhyme. Illustrations (as necessary) can be drawn on individual 3-x-5-inch index cards.

Provide a small group of children with the 20 cards turned facedown. Invite one child to turn over two cards. If the two cards have the same beginning sound, the player keeps the cards and gets to take another turn. If the two cards do not have the same beginning sound, the child turns over the cards and the next player takes a turn. The winner is the player with the most sets of cards at the end.

9 Select several three-phoneme words from a current piece of children's literature you are sharing with the class. Using several strips of masking tape make a rectangle (approximately 2 feet x 6 feet) on the floor of the classroom. Further divide the rectangle into three 2-x-2-foot boxes as in the illustration below.

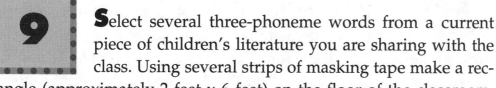

Stand at one end of the rectangle and say one of the three-phoneme words. Invite the children to repeat the word after you. Then tell the children that you will say the word again, except this time you will say it slowly and hop into each box for each sound in the word. For example:

The word is *bike*:
- You say bike.
- Students repeat, saying *bike*.
- You say /b/ and hop into the first square.
- You say /i/ and hop into the second square.
- You say /k/ and hop into the third square.

The word is *phone*:
- You say *phone*.
- Students repeat, saying *phone*.
- You say /f/ and hop into the first square.
- You say /o/ and hop into the second square.
- You say /n/ and hop into the third square.

Variation: Invite the children to hop into each square as you say the individual phonemes of selected three-phoneme words. When the children are comfortable with that part of the activity, invite them to repeat it in pairs, with two children holding hands and hopping together through the squares.

10 **V**isit a local toy store or variety store. Purchase a quantity of "crickets" or "clickers" (small hand-held devices with a straight piece of metal or plastic that is pressed down with the thumb to create a noticeable "click" or "pop"). Provide one "cricket" for each child in the class.

Obtain a variety of small objects, each of which has two, three, or four phonemes in its name. Place these objects in a grocery bag. Invite one child to remove an object from the bag and say its name. Encourage the class to click their "crickets" as they repeat the word and say each sound in the object's name.

11 **S**elect several words from a piece of children's litera-ture you are sharing with the class (it is advisable to begin this activity with several one-syllable words). Place three or four children in a row (in chairs) in the front of the classroom. Stand to the right of the first child in the row. Tell the chil-dren that you will say a word that has several sounds in it, but you

over the top of a table or desk. Tell the children that they are going on a fishing trip with you. You will say a target word. Invite a child to use her or his "fishing pole" to pick up one of the "fish" on the table. Have the child check the number on the "fish" and to say the sound from the target word corresponding to its position in the word. For example, the target word is *duck*:

• Say the word *duck*.

• Invite a child to pick up a "fish."

• Encourage the child to say the number on the "fish" (for example, 1).

• Invite the child to say the middle sound in the target word (the number 2 represents the middle sound; 1 is the beginning sound; and 3 is the ending sound).

• The child will say /u/.

Here's another example:

• Say the word *tree*.

• Invite a child to pick up a "fish."

• Encourage the child to say the number on the "fish" (for example, 1).

• Invite the child to say the first sound in the target word.

• The child will say /t/.

will say it very slowly. For each sound you will stand behind an individual child seated on the chairs. For example:

The word is *dog*:
• You say /d/ (while standing behind the first child in the row).
• You say /o/ (move and stand behind the second child in the row).
• You say /g/ (move and stand behind the third child in the row).

The word is *card*:
• You say /k/ (while standing behind the first child in the row).
• You say /ar/ (move and stand behind the second child in the row).
• You say /d/ (move and stand behind the third child in the row).

Hint: This activity works particularly well when children have an opportunity to select several words from a book being read to them. Invite them to suggest some words and then select several one-syllable (three- or four-phoneme) words from the list they dictate.

Variation: As the children become familiar and comfortable with this activity, invite one to stand with you behind the row of seated individuals. Stand behind the child and place your hands on her or his shoulders. Help that child move with you as you say a selected word. Invite several individuals to participate in this physical segmentation activity.

12 Invite the entire class to stand up. Tell the children that you will say some words to them, one at a time. Instruct them to place both hands on the sides of their heads when they hear the first sound in each word. Tell them to place both hands on their waists when they hear the middle sound in each word. Tell them to put their hands on their feet when they hear the ending sound in each word. (*Note:* This activity requires the use of three-phoneme words only.) Here are some examples:

Book: /b/ (hands on head); /oo/ (hands on waist); /k/ (hands on toes)
Cake: /k/ (hands on head); /a/ (hands on waist); /k/ (hands on toes)
Tub: /t/ (hands on head); /u/ (hands on waist); /b/ (hands on toes)
Pig: /p/ (hands on head); /i/ (hands on waist); /g/ (hands on toes)

13 Provide several small teams of children with four small inexpensive bar magnets each. Tell the children that you will say a word and that they are to repeat it back to you. As they repeat the word, they are to place a magnet on a table for each sound they hear in the word. For example, you say *baby*. Children repeat the word and:

- Place one bar magnet down for the /b/ sound.
- Place another bar magnet down for the /a/ sound.
- Place a third bar magnet down for the /be/ sound.

Invite the children to repeat each target word by sweeping a finger across the magnets, touching each one as each sound in the word is said. This activity works best with two-, three-, or four-phoneme words selected from a nursery rhyme or children's book.

Note: This activity is quite instructive because as children put down each magnet, the magnets will be attracted to each other (depending on their polarity). Children begin to see how sounds are "attracted" or "linked" to each other to form units we know as words.

14 Draw a picture of a train locomotive, several passenger cars, and a caboose on a sheet of construction paper (or trace the following illustration). Cut out the individual objects and put a small hook and loop fastener dot on the back of each one. Place the corresponding hook and loop fastener on the chalkboard or a large sheet of oaktag on which you have drawn a train track.

Tell the children to listen carefully to a word you say and to watch as you place a part of the train on the board or sheet of oaktag. Tell them that you will place the locomotive on the board when you

say the first sound in a word. You will place a passenger car (one or two) after the locomotive for the middle sound(s) in a word. And, you will place the caboose on the board for the ending sound in a word.

Variations:

- Invite the children to repeat each word with you. At the same time, point to each train car to identify the first, middle, and ending sounds in the target word. When the children are comfortable with this procedure, reverse the activity and remove the locomotive as you say the first sound, the passenger car(s) as you say the middle sound(s), and the caboose as you say the ending sound.

- Invite individual children to come to the front of the room. Say a target word and encourage a child to place each train car on the board to represent the beginning, middle, and ending sounds of the word.

- Prepare sufficient quantities of the train cars so that each child in the class has a collection. Repeat the activity above, inviting all the children to participate at the same time.

15 Draw and cut out several paper fish from a sheet of construction paper. On one-third of the "fish," write the number 1. On another third, write the number 2. On the final third of the "fish," write the number 3. Place a small piece of magnetic tape on the back of each "fish."

Provide selected individuals in the class with a straw onto which has been tied a magnet on a length of string. Spread the magnetic fish

Stage 5: Sound Manipulation Activities

1 **T**ell the children that throughout the course of the day you will use their names—but that you will remove the first sound in each name you use (for example, change "Yolanda" to "Olanda" or change "Dennis" to "Ennis.").

During the course of a following day, tell the children that you will say their names, but this time you will remove the ending sound in each name you use (for example, change "Yolanda" to "Yoland" or change "Dennis" to "Denni").

Hint: Just for fun, I tell children that they can manipulate my last name and refer to me throughout the day by my "new name." For example, they can call me Mr. Redericks (initial sound deletion) or Mr. Frederick (final sound deletion).

2 **P**ost an Animal Picture Card (see pages 199–203) at the top of the chalkboard. Tell the children that you are going to teach them a new game. In this game, they will say the name of the animal represented by a specific card. Then, you will tell them to do something unusual and funny with that word. Here are some examples:

Animal Picture Card: bat
You: What's this word?
Children: *Bat*.
You: Say *bat* without the /b/ (initial sound deletion).
Children: /at/
You: Say *bat* without the /t/ (final sound deletion).
Children: /ba/

Animal Picture Card: mouse
You: What's this word?
Children: *Mouse*.
You: Say *mouse* without the /m/ (initial sound deletion).
Children: /ouse/

You: Say *mouse* without the /s/ (final sound deletion).
Children: /mou/

Animal Picture Card: snake

You: What's this word?
Children: *Snake.*
You: Say *snake* without the /s/ (initial sound deletion).
Children: /nake/
You: Say *snake* without the /k/ (final sound deletion).
Children: /sna/

3 **O**btain an old magazine. Cut out several large pictures and paste each picture to a sheet of construction paper. Divide the class into several small groups and provide each group with one picture. Tell the children that you will say the name of an object that is in one of the pictures; however, you will say the name without its first sound. The children in each group must look carefully at all the items in their picture and identify the single item with the missing sound.

For example, in an advertisement for a car (which is driving along a country road with lots of trees along the sides), you might say "I see a /oad/." Children would look at the picture and try to identify the word as *road*. You might say "I see a /ire/." Children would look at the picture and identify the word as *tire*.

Hint: Create a file of dozens of these picture sheets. This can then be used as a quick "filler" activity whenever you've completed a lesson early or when you have a few extra minutes while the children are waiting for music class, gym, or library time to begin.

4 **T**ell children that you are going to create some rhyming riddles for them. You will say a word and they are to think of a word that rhymes with your word and begins with an identified sound. Select words from the Rhyming Picture Cards (see pages 190–198) to create your riddles. For example:

> You: I'm thinking of a word that rhymes with *bag* and starts with /w/.
> Children: *Wag*.

> You: I'm thinking of a word that rhymes with *hen* and starts with /m/.
> Children: *Men*.

> You: I'm thinking of a word that rhymes with *well* and starts with /b/.
> Children: *Bell*.

> You: I'm thinking of a word that rhymes with *king* and starts with /r/.
> Children: *Ring*.

Hint: This is a great "filler" activity that can be done two minutes before recess, just before lunch, or while in line waiting for dismissal.

5 **T**each children the words and music to the song "The Itsy Bitsy Spider." When children are comfortable with the song, tell them that you are going to create some new words by substituting the initial sound in some words with new sounds. Sing the new song for the children and invite them to sing along with you. Here are two examples:

> The itsy bitsy spider
> Climbed up the water spout
> Down came the rain
> And washed the spider out
> Out came the sun
> And dried up all the rain
> And the itsy bitsy spider
> Climbed up the spout again.

The *mitsy mitsy* spider	The *ritsy ritsy* spider
Climbed up the water spout	Climbed up the water spout
Down came the rain	Down came the rain
And washed the spider out	And washed the spider out
Out came the sun	Out came the sun
And dried up all the rain	And dried up all the rain
And the *mitsy mitsy* spider	And the *ritsy ritsy* spider
Climbed up the spout again.	Climbed up the spout again.

Variation: Invite the children to suggest other familiar songs in which selected words can have their initial sounds replaced with other sounds. For example:

Jimmy Cracked Corn

Rimmy racked rorn, and I ron't rare
Rimmy racked rorn, and I ron't rare
Rimmy racked rorn and I ron't rare
Ry raster's ronn away.

Post a Rhyming Picture Card at the top of the chalkboard. Tell the children that you are going to help them create some new words just by removing the beginning sound in the target word (the card posted).

For example, put the picture card for *ham* at the top of the board. Invite children to take away the first sound of the word (/h/) and replace it with /r/. What new word do they have? (*ram*) Then, take away the first sound of the word *ham* (/h/) and replace it with a /j/. What new word do they have? (*jam*)

Hint: You'll discover that almost all the Rhyming Picture Card families can be used for this fun and enjoyable activity.

7 **W**rite initial consonant sounds on several index cards, one sound per card. Place all the cards in a brown lunch bag. At the beginning of the day, invite one child to reach into the bag and select one card. Identify the sound for the children and then tell them that during the course of the day you will say each of their names using the identified sound as the beginning sound for each name. For example:

/m/: Barry becomes *Marry*
Sandra becomes *Mandra*
Jose becomes *Mose*
Carla becomes *Marla*

/r/: Barry becomes *Rarry*
Sandra becomes *Randra*
Jose becomes *Rose*
Carla becomes *Rarla*

/d/: Barry becomes *Darry*
Sandra becomes *Dandra*
Jose becomes *Dose*
Carla becomes *Darla*

Invite children to use their "new names" throughout the day (a few gentle reminders about the target sound may be necessary). They may wish to refer to themselves and each other by their "new names."

Variation: Invite the children to select a favorite nursery rhyme. Share the nursery rhyme together as a class. Then modify as many words as possible by substituting the "Sound of the Day" in place of initial letters. Read the revised nursery rhyme for the class.

8 **S**elect one of the Animal Picture Cards and post it at the top of the chalkboard. Tell the children that you are going to play a fun game with them and create some new and unusual animals. You are going to make those animals by changing the first sound at the beginning of the name of a familiar animal.

For example, post the Animal Picture Card of a goat at the top of the chalkboard. Say the word for the children; then, say it again, this time substituting another consonant in place of the *g* (*t*, for example). Tell the children that you have just created a brand new animal (a "toat"). Say the name of the new "animal" and draw an imaginary picture of this fictitious creature.

Repeat with other beginning consonants to create additional fictitious creatures. For each "creature" draw an illustration (artistic talent is not necessary—the wilder and crazier the better). Here are some imaginary creatures you could create from the target word *goat*:

Toat   **Zoat**   **Noat**

Doat   **Joat**

Repeat this activity with additional Animal Picture Cards.

Variations:

• After doing the activity above, invite the class to select an Animal Picture card. This is posted at the top of the chalkboard. Encourage them to change the sound at the beginning of the depicted word/picture in order to create a new word. Draw an imaginary animal for the new creation.

• When the children are comfortable with this activity, invite them to create the names of imaginary creatures (which you will draw) by replacing the *last* letter of an animal's name with another letter.

9 **D**uplicate the Rhyming Picture Cards onto heavy card stock. Laminate and cut them apart. Shuffle them and provide each child with one card. Arrange the children in a circle in the middle of the room. Tap one child to begin the activity.

The child says the name of the object on the card. She or he then turns to the person on the left and says, "(Word), (Word), make a new word!" The person on the left must delete the initial sound and replace it with a new sound to create a new word. Then, that person identifies the object on her or his card, turns to the person on the left, and says, "(Word), (Word), make a new word!" The process continues around the circle until everyone has had an opportunity to create a new word and share her or his word. For example:

> You: Tammy, what is your word?
> Tammy: *Drum.* Drum, Drum, make a new word!
> Raphael: *Gum.* My word is *Bank.* Bank, Bank, make a
> new word!
> T.J.: *Tank.* My word is *Meat.* Meat, Meat, make a new word!
> Addie: *Heat.* My word is *Rice.* Rice, Rice, make a new word!
> Jimmy: *Mice.* My word is *Hose.* Hose, Hose, make a
> new word!

Literature-Based Activities

Anna Banana: 101 Jump-Rope Rhymes

by Joanna Cole
New York: Morrow Junior Books, 1989

Summary: This book contains 101 rhyming poems for children to enjoy, both jump roping and just chanting. Phonemic awareness abounds in this book. You will find that many of the children already know many of these rhymes as well as the accompanying melodies.

Activity: Just for fun, introduce a "Rhyme a Day" to the children. If some students in your class already know a rhyme, invite them to teach it to the rest of the class. If possible, you may wish to invite selected individuals to demonstrate a rhyme using a jump rope. Be sure to emphasize the lyrical nature of each rhyme as well as the wide variety of rhyming words.

Note: One teacher I know begins each day with a selected rhyme from this book. The rhyme may be a new one or one with which students are already familiar. This puts students in a poetic frame of mind at the beginning of the day and lets them know that rhyming and singing are a natural part of the learning process, just as they are of the reading process.

Activity: Select a jump rope rhyme from the book. Instruct students on how to clap the rhyme as they sing it, one clap for each syllable. If necessary, you may wish to slow down the speed of the rhyme initially in order for students to "keep the pace." Once students are used to the pace and rhythm of a rhyme, you may wish to speed it up a little more each time you share it with students.

Barn Dance

by Bill Martin, Jr.,
and John Archambault
New York: Henry Holt and Company, 1986

Summary: On a moonlit night, a young boy has trouble sleeping. As he looks out his window, he hears a night owl beckon him to come closer and join in the fun. This is a delightful story of the unexpected when a young boy finds himself dancing with the animals while everyone else is sleeping.

Activity: Read each set of words below. Invite children to tell you which word in each set does not belong with the rest of the words in the set.

sleep, sheep, kids
night, begin, right
bed, low, so

round, field, sound
rockin, stockin, fiddle
grab, crow, bow

Activity: Invite children to listen to the following divided words from the story. Encourage them to combine the sounds and say the words created from each combination.

rab–bit
farm–house
scare–crow
hoe–down

wel–come
barn–yard
tip–toed

Activity: Say each word in the following sets. Invite students to identify the words that do and do not begin with the same sound. What is the common sound? What is the sound that is different?

farmer, fiddle, moon
kid, cow, partner
show, curtsy, crow

tucked, skinny, tune
bed, head, begin
barrel, barnyard, pink

Barnyard Banter

by Denise Fleming
New York: Henry Holt and Company, 1994

Summary: As the day starts on the farm, the animals are going about their business making the usual animal noises. But where is goose? In this delightfully colorful book, children are introduced to the usual clucking, mewing, and cooing of a rich and varied barnyard. This book lends itself to lots of audience participation and classroom fun.

Activity: Tell students you are going to show them how some words can be separated into two different parts. Inform students that you will select several words from the book. You will say the first part of the word, then the second part of the word. They are to listen carefully and put the two parts of each word together to form a complete word. Here are some words you can use:

/m/ /oo/	/p/ /igs/	/m/ /uck/	/cr/ /ows/
/fr/ /og/	/m/ /ew/	/w/ /ire/	/w/ /all/
/h/ /ens/	/sq/ /ueak/	/h/ /onk/	/st/ /one/
/cl/ /uck/	/m/ /ice/	/c/ /ow/	/p/ /ond/

Activity: After students have heard the story several times, invite them to repeat it along with you as follows: Work with the art teacher to create a series of drawings of all of the barnyard animals. Duplicate multiple copies of each drawing and glue each one to the end of a craft stick. Make enough so that every child has an animal from the story. Read the story aloud, and when the sounds are made, invite the students holding a particular animal's picture to make the sound and wave their animal in the air.

As a variation, repeat the activity above, and when it comes time for the sound made by each animal, invite youngsters to make a rhyming sound (imaginary or real).

Brown Bear Brown Bear, What Do You See?

by Bill Martin, Jr.
Orlando, Florida: Harcourt Brace and Company, 1970

Summary: Simply put, this is a book that should be in every teacher's classroom. Filled with imaginative and colorful illustrations by Eric Carle and a lilting and engaging verse by Bill Martin, Jr., this book stands as a classic of children's literature. It's a story that can be read over and over again—and one that will constantly delight. A variety of animals are asked a basic question ("What do you see?"), and the reader is led through a succession of colorful creatures with verse that begs to be sung. This book is a staple of any reading program.

Activity: After students are familiar with the story, invite them to assist you in creating a new story. For the new version, each color must be followed by the name of an animal that starts with the same sound as the animal's name. Here are some possibilities to get you started:

Brown bull, brown bull
Red rooster, red rooster
Yellow yak, yellow yak
Blue bee, blue bee
Gray goose, gray goose
Green gopher, green gopher
Purple parrot, purple parrot
Pink porcupine, pink porcupine
White whale, white whale
Black bug, black bug
Gold gorilla, gold gorilla

Sing the new version along with the children. Invite them to contribute new animal names over an extended period of time. You may wish to create large picture cards of each new animal and post these across the chalkboard for a new reading of the book (inviting students to say the story along with you).

Activity: Invite students to modify the story by creating some rhyming phrases, each of which uses a selected animal from the book. Here are some examples:

Brown bear, brown bear, what do you *wear?*
Redbird, redbird, what have you *heard?*
Yellow duck, yellow duck, hope you had some *luck.*
Blue horse, blue horse, did you run the *course?*
Gray mouse, gray mouse, do you have a *house?*

Activity: Obtain some 5-x-8-inch index cards. On each one draw an illustration of one of the animals from the book. Select one of the cards and say the name of the animal for the children. Post the card on the chalkboard. Demonstrate for children how the word for that picture can be used to create a silly sentence, a sentence in which every word begins with the same sound. For example, if you placed an illustration of a bear on the board, you might create the following sentence: "Brown bears begin bumping bugs." Be sure to point out to children the fact that each word in a sentence begins with the same sound. Create additional alliterative sentences for other animals in the book and say them for your students. Here are a few to get you started:

Redbirds run rapidly.
Ducks do delightful dances.
Hairy horses help hide holes.
Merry mouse makes music.
Frantic frogs feel fine.

Chicka Chicka Boom Boom

by Bill Martin, Jr.,
and John Archambault
New York: Simon and Schuster, Inc., 1989

Summary: A delightful book of rhyming and repetition as the letters of the alphabet try to climb a coconut tree. Finally, too many letters are in the tree and they all fall down. Rescued by their parents and relatives, the letters are dusted off and patched up. It's not too long, however, before they discover the tree again and the sequence starts back up once more. Full of fun and full of colorful characters, this book is emblematic of the quality of Bill Martin's work.

Activity: Read the following sets of words (or letters) from the book. Invite students to listen carefully and to note the word in each set that does not belong with the others.

> C, tree, meet, D
> boom, room, doot
> K, way, will
> P, T, R, V
> cry, tie, fly, way
> E, G, I, free

Activity: Read the following words from the book to the children. Invite the children to tell you the beginning sound at the start of the words in each set.

> comes, coconut, catch
> top, tree, toe
> beat, boom, breath
> way, will
> flip, flop, flee

Each Peach Pear Plum

by Janet and Allan Ahlberg
New York: Viking, 1978

Summary: In a rhythmic lilting verse the narrator spies several different story-book characters ranging from Tom Thumb to the Three Bears. The reader is invited to search for the characters in the illustration accompanying each page. Eventually, at the end of the book, *everyone* is located. This is an ideal read-along, follow-along book for youngsters. Full of fun and full of surprises, children will enjoy hearing this book again and again.

Activity: Say: Listen to the following word from the story. I will say it in two parts. Put the parts together to make a whole word: Hub . . . bard. What's the word? (Hubbard) Now, I will do the same thing for some other words in the story. I will say the two parts of each word and you put the two parts together and say the whole word.

cel ... lar	bunt ... ing	wick ... ed
hunt ... ing	a ... sleep	rob ... in

Say the two parts of each word above. Invite children to repeat the complete word each time.

Activity: Listen to these three words from the story. Which words do not begin with the same sound: *pear, plum, Tom?* Here are some other groups of words from the story. Choose which word in each group does not begin with the same sound as the other two words:

spy, stairs, three	spy, Jack, Jill	safe, dry, spy

Activity: Say: I'm going to make up some new sentences. I'll use a word from the story and then add new words. Listen carefully and tell me the sound you hear at the beginning of each word in a sentence:

Patty picks peaches.	Babies break bottles.
Big bad bears.	Jill jumps joyfully.

Four Fur Feet

by Margaret Wise Brown
New York: Hyperion Books for Children,
1994

Summary: In a repetitive cumulative story, a mysterious creature takes a journey on his four fur feet around the world. The primary phrases are repeated over and over again, encouraging active participation on the part of any young audience. Children will delight in hearing the /f/ sound over and over as the last sound in each paragraph.

Activity: Say the phrase "four fur feet" to the children. Ask them to say it back to you. Invite them to notice that each word begins with the same sound (/f/). This is called *alliteration.* Work with students to create additional alliterative phrases, using parts of their own bodies or parts of the bodies of animals. For example:

Human Body	Animal Body
nifty neat nose	five fantastic fangs
ten tough teeth	heavy hairy horns
furry flashy fingers	cute cuddly claws
ten tingly toes	ten terrific tentacles
big beautiful bones	wild wonderful wings
healthy happy hips	totally terrific tail
large lumpy legs	fluffy flashy fur

Activity: Tell students that you are going to play a fun game with them. As you reread the story to them, stretch out the beginning sound in several selected words. For example: "Then he w-w-w-w-w-w-walked into the country. . . ." Invite students to tell you the sound at the beginning of each stretched word.

Fox in Socks

by Dr. Seuss
New York: Random House, 1965

Summary: A delightful book of rhymes and tongue twisters.

Activity: Invite the children to listen to each set of words below and tell you what they hear in the middle of the words. What is the same about the middle of each of these words?

fox, socks, box, knox	game, lame, shame
chick, brick, trick, quick	new, blue, glue, chew
clock, block, stock, tock	cheese, freeze, sneeze, breeze
rose, hose, nose, goes	

Activity: Invite the children to listen to each set of words below. Encourage them to tell you the two rhyming words in each set. Which word does not rhyme with the other two?

sick, tick, tock	puddle, paddle, muddle,
goes, sews, glue	rubber, tweetle, beetle
blibber, blubber, rubber	noodle, blibber, poodle
please, fleas, band	muddled, duddled, please
blew, bang, glue	

Activity: Invite children to listen to the following alliterative sentences. Encourage them to repeat each sentence after you. Ask them to identify the beginning sound in all the words in a sentence.

Sue sews Sue's socks.	Ben's bent broom breaks.
Bim brings Ben's broom.	Bim's bent broom breaks.
Ben brings Bim's broom.	Luke Luck likes lakes.
Ben bends Bim's broom.	Luke Luck licks lakes.
Bim bends Ben's broom.	

In the Tall, Tall Grass

by Denise Fleming
New York: Henry Holt and Company, 1991

Summary: This is a delightful book that begs to be read aloud. An array of creatures, a melody of sounds, and a variety of activities take place in the tall, tall grass. Colorful and bright illustrations highlight this ideal book for any classroom library. This is a book teachers will read over and over and one that children will request over and over.

Activity: This book lends itself to lots of rhyming activities. For this activity, repeat each pair of words that appears on a two-page spread (such as *strum* and *drum*). Invite youngsters to contribute one more word that rhymes with one or both of those two words. Here are some possibilities:

crunch, munch, *bunch*   pull, tug, *rug*
cart, dip, *trip*   slip, slide, *ride*
crack, snap, *rap*

Activity: Inform students that you are going to work with them to create some "Karate Words." These are words you have selected from the book and are going to "chop" in half. To begin, you will say a word. Then, you will give the word an imaginary "karate chop" (to divide it into two parts). Then you will say one of the two parts and invite students to tell you the other (missing) part of the word. For example:

You: *Slip.*   You: *Zap.*   You: *Flop.*
You: /sl/   You: /z/   You: /fl/
Students: /ip/   Students: /ap/   Students: /op/
Students: *Slip.* Students: *Zap.*   Students: *Flop.*

I Went Walking

by Sue Williams
San Diego: Gulliver Books, 1969

Summary: A young boy takes a walk and discovers that different creatures of many colors live in the world around him. This book will delight children with its colorful illustrations and rhythmic text. This book would be an ideal companion to Bill Martin's book *Brown Bear, Brown Bear, What Do You See?*

Activity: After reading the book to children, tell them that you will read it again, but that you will eliminate the last sentence in each stanza. Their job is to suggest an appropriate sentence (either the original one or another) for the missing one. Here is an example: "I went walking. What did you see? I saw a green duck *bouncing on my knee.*"

Activity: Invite the children to blend together the sounds that you say to make the following words:

/d/ /o/ /g/
/h/ /or/ /s/
/c/ /ow/
/p/ /i/ /g/
/d/ /u/ /k/
/c/ /a/ /t/

Activity: Tell students that you will "rubber band" (stretch out the sounds) some of the words from the book. You may wish to loop a rubber band around the index finger on each hand and physically stretch it out in front of your lips as you say each word. Here are some possible "rubber band" words:

w–e–n–t	r–e–d
d–i–d	c–ow
b–l–a–ck	d–u–ck
c–a–t	p–i–g
b–r–ow–n	d–o–g
h–or–se	

Noisy Nora

by Rosemary Wells
New York: Dial Books for Young Readers,
1973

Summary: Nora is feeling sorry for herself. No one is paying attention to her, so to gain attention Nora begins making noise—lots of noise! She bangs the window, drops her sister's marbles, and knocks down the lamp. Still nobody notices her. Finally, she announces that she's leaving. It's then that everyone begins to appreciate noisy Nora. This book is full of fun and magical illustrations. It's an ideal book for making lots of sounds—both loud and soft.

Activity: The following words all come from the story. Read them to the children and invite them to notice the beginning sound at the start of each word in a set.

filthy, fell, flew   song, stopped, sister
down, dumb, dinner   burping, banged, brother

Invite youngsters to contribute a new word to each set—a word that begins with the same sound as the other words in the set.

Activity: Obtain some craft sticks. Color some of them red, some yellow, and some green. Distribute the sticks to children in the class (each child will have one of each color). Inform students that you will ask them some questions. Let them know beforehand that you will select a word from the story and ask them to locate a specific sound within each word. The sounds in each word will be at the start, middle, or end of a word. If they hear the sound at the beginning of the word, they are to hold up their red sticks. If the sound is in the middle of the word, they are to hold up their yellow sticks. And, if the sound is at the end of the word, they are to hold up their green sticks.

Where is the /k/ in the word *Kate?*
Where is the /ai/ in the word *wait?*
Where is the /k/ in the word *back?*
Where is the /e/ in the word *needed?*
Where is the /r/ in the word *hear?*
Where is the /b/ in the word *tub?*

One Fish Two Fish, Red Fish Blue Fish

by Dr. Seuss
New York: Random House, Inc., 1976

Summary: This book brings a whole new light to silliness in rhymes. Every turn of the page is filled with a plethora of rhyming letter combinations.

Activity: Select several words from the book. Read each of these words to the children. Invite students to identify the first part (onset) of each word. Then, invite students to identify the second part (rime) of each word. The following words can be used:

bump	yell
bed	drink
dear	cow
gold	fish
hook	

Activity: Select specific passages from the book and read them aloud to students. Invite students to identify the rhyming words in each passage. Afterward, encourage students to alter each passage by substituting new rhyming words (real or made up) in place of the ones currently in the text.

Polar Bear, Polar Bear, What Do You Hear?

by Bill Martin, Jr., and Eric Carle
New York: Henry Holt and Company, 1991

Summary: Using the repetitive line "What do you hear?", each animal answers the question with another animal. This cumulative, rhythmic tale continues to delight children with its bright lyrics and equally bright illustrations. This book is a staple in many primary classrooms around the country.

Activity: After you have read this book to the children, reread it, changing the lines to include the names of students in the class. Invite each named student to contribute a new "vocalization" for each last line. For example:

Theodore, Theodore, what do you hear?
I hear a lion (*roaring*) in my ear.

Sarah Jean, Sarah Jean, what do you hear?
I hear a zebra (*crying*) in my ear.

Laura, Laura, what do you hear?
I hear an elephant (*singing*) in my ear.

Activity: Invite the children to continue the story by adding their own animals to the text. Encourage children to add new animals along with their representative sounds. Here are some examples:

Shark, Shark, what do you hear?
I hear a monkey laughing in my ear.

Monkey, Monkey, what do you hear?
I hear a snail whispering in my ear.

Snail, snail, what do you hear?
I hear a chicken peeping in my ear.

Plan some time to focus on the two major rhyming words (*hear–ear*) that are repeated throughout the book.

Roar and More

by Karla Kuskin
New York: Harper and Row, 1990

Summary: Using rhymes, Karla Kuskin depicts different animals and some of the sounds they make. Each animal has a completed poem that describes their habits, likes and dislikes, and habitats. Each animal and each poem stands alone, or they can all be combined into a single reading.

Activity: Read the following sets of words from the book to the children. Invite the students to listen carefully and note any similarities within a group of words.

> jump, wump, thrump
> kangaroo, true, two, new
> flowers, powers, hours

Afterward, read each set of words to students again. Now, invite them to add one more word to each set (a real or imaginary word) that rhymes with the other words in the set.

Activity: Read the following words to students, one at a time.

full	fall
bone	jump
mat	fish
wish	dog
run	bark
bee	feet
walls	keep

Tell students that you will remove the first sound in the first word and replace that sound with a new sound. The addition of the new sound will create a new word. For example, remove the first sound from *full* to create /ull/. Add the /b/ sound to create a new word, *bull*. Do the same thing with the other words in the list. After students understand the procedure, invite them to add a new sound to the beginning of those words to create their own new words.

Sheep in a Jeep

by Nancy Shaw
Boston: Houghton Mifflin, 1986

Summary: In a rollicking, rhyming story, the saga of several sheep and their efforts to maneuver a jeep down a hill and through a mudhole is hilariously presented and illustrated in this fun book. Part of an imaginative series that relies on few words to carry the action, this entry will have kids begging for more *Sheep* books and listening to the playful ways in which the author has skillfully manipulated language.

Activity: Read the book out loud to your students, page by page. Track the print as you read. Invite students to locate the two rhyming words on each page. After identifying the two rhyming words on each page, reread the page with an extra emphasis on the rhyming words. Invite students to say the rhyming words along with you (with extra emphasis) as you read a page through for a third time.

Activity: After reading the book to your students, read the following sets of words out loud. Invite children to listen to each set and tell you what they hear in the middle of each word in a set. What is the same about the middle of each of the following groups of three words?

sheep, jeep, beep	weep, steep, heap
leap, steep, jeep	sweep, cheap, steep
deep, beep, sheep	

Reread the story and invite children to raise their hands when they hear any one of the words listed above.

Activity: Read each of the following words to children. Invite them to say each word back to you. Then, ask them to say each word again without the ending sound. For example: a) You say *jeep*, b) the children say *jeep*, and c) the children say *jee*.

beep	look	shout
hill	mud	sweep

Invite youngsters to repeat this activity. After they say each word without its ending sound, ask them to identify the missing sound.

Sheep Out to Eat

by Nancy Shaw
Boston: Houghton Mifflin, 1992

Summary: Rhyming abounds in this funny story about five hungry sheep that decide to stop at an old fashioned tea shop for something to eat. As they innocently destroy the place, they find that this might not be the right location to satisfy their hunger. This book is another hilarious and fun-to-read book in the *Sheep* series by Nancy Shaw. Simplistic language and rollicking good times abound in the entire series—certainly a positive addition to any read-aloud activities for young students.

Activity: Read each of the following words to children. Invite them to say each word back to you. Then ask them to say each word again without the beginning sound. For example: a) You say *sheep*, b) the children say *sheep*, and c) the children say _eep_.

stop	read
small	soup
seat	scoop
bite	slurp
feed	burp
point	bites
lose	cake
jump	bump
tips	dishes

Activity: After reading the book to your students, read the following pairs of words out loud. Invite children to listen to each pair of words and tell you what they hear at the end of each word in a pair. What is the same sound at the end of each word in the following pairs of words?

sheep–stop	waiter–pepper
seat–bite	sneeze–knees
get–want	smash–crash
word–read	break–cake
soup–sheep	mop–sheep
add–custard	lip–tip

Summary: In this story, all kinds of animals fall into the water for different reasons. And when they do . . . the noises that they make! Children will enjoy the humor and colorful illustrations as they listen to this rhyming book.

> # Splash, Splash
> by Jeff Sheppard
> New York: Macmillan Publishing Company, 1994

Activity: Invite the children to listen to the following sets of words and tell you what is the same in these words:

buzz–does	understand–land
surprise–eyes	all–small
cake–lake	feet–sweet
then–again	playing–saying
grim–swim	

Activity: Invite the children to listen to the following sets of words:

cake, lake
feet, sweet
grim, swim

Encourage children to delete the first sound in each word and say the remaining sounds. Then, invite them to add different sounds to the beginning of the words to create new words.

Activity: Write several of the words that can be illustrated with pictures (bee, cat, dog), each on an individual 5-x-8-inch index card. Post one card at the top of the chalkboard. Tell students that you are going to help them create some real words and silly words just by removing the beginning sound in the target word (the card posted).

For example, put the *mouse* picture card at the top of the board. Invite students to take away the first sound of the word (/m/) and replace it with a /h/. What new word do they have? (*house*) Then take away the first sound of the *mouse* picture card (/m/) and replace it with an /l/. What new word do they have? (*louse*)

The Z Was Zapped

by Chris Van Allsburg
Boston: Houghton Mifflin, 1987

Summary: This is a very funny story about the different letters of the alphabet and the disasters that happen to them. Children will love the adventure as they travel through the alphabet waiting for the disaster.

Activity: Invite children to clap out the number of syllables in the capitalized words used with each of the letters of the alphabet. For example:

av–a–lanche (3 claps)
bit–ten (2 claps)
cut (1 clap)
drowned (1 clap)
e–vap–or–a–ting (5 claps)
flat–ten–ed (3 claps)

Activity: Reread the story to the students. Invite the children to think of words that start with each letter of the alphabet. Encourage children to change the disaster word and replace it with another word that starts with the same sound. Invite the children to say the sentences with their new words in them. For example, "The *G* was starting to Grumble," or "The *H* was somewhat Helpless."

Activity: Create new rhyming sentences using the letters of the alphabet. Invite the children to pick out the rhyming words in each sentence. Here are some to get you started:

A likes to make clay.   *I* have a sty.
It is the *B*, I can see.   *J* likes to play.
D had to flee.   *T* floats in the sea.

Later invite children to replace the last word with a different word that would rhyme with the letter (for example, *A* likes to make hay . . . *clay* is replaced by *hay*).

A Selected Bibliography

The following books offer you several opportunities to share phonemic awareness skills in context. In other words, children will have the chance to hear the sounds of language in meaningful and age-appropriate literature. By making these books a regular part of your classroom program, you will be assisting children in developing appropriate listening skills, positive attitudes toward reading, and a knowledge of the utility of phonemic awareness in pleasurable texts. As you read these books to your students, consider the following options as positive adjuncts to your phonemic awareness program:

- Read and reread a book several times. Make sure children hear the joy and magic of reading in your voice each time.

- After you have read a selected book several times, invite children to comment about the selection. For example: "Did you enjoy the books? Was it fun? What was fun about it?"

- As appropriate, model some metacognitive behaviors. For example: "Wow, that was a funny part!" or "I liked the way the author made that part rhyme." or "It was interesting how the character got all mixed up there."

- Encourage youngsters to make predictions during follow-up readings of a familiar book. For example, you may start off by reading, "The farmer had a *flood* that filled his barn with _____." Invite children to suggest possible words to fill in the blank.

- Invite children to examine language use. This is particularly appropriate after children have heard a story several times. You can start this off with comments such as, "It looks like the author begins all these words with the same sound. What did you notice about those three words? What sounds the same in the sentence I just read?"

- Encourage youngsters to create additional verses on their own. They may wish to invent a sequel to a story or create a silly rhyme to play off of a familiar line. Encourage lots of language play with a playful silly attitude, and children will begin to understand the inherent fun in all types of language use.

This bibliography is not meant to be a finite list. You are encouraged to add to this list as new books are published and as new titles become available. Solicit recommendations from friends and colleagues and consider these selections as important components of any phonemic awareness program.

Aardema, V. (1981). *Bringing the Rain to Kapiti Plain.* New York: Dial. Using the format of "This Is the House That Jack Built," the author weaves an engaging tale that stimulates active participation for any young audience.

Ahlberg, J., & Ahlberg, A. (1978). *Each Peach Pear Plum.* New York: Viking. Readers are invited to play "I Spy" with a variety of characters from various Mother Goose rhymes.

Alborough, J. (1994). *Where's My Teddy?* Cambridge, MA: Candlewick. A small boy goes searching for a lost teddy bear in the woods and makes a surprising discovery.

Barchas, S. (1989). *I Was Walking Down the Road.* New York: Scholastic. In a comic strip format, rhyming words and sequencing are introduced to young readers.

Bayer, J. (1984). *A My Name Is Alice.* New York: Dial. Each letter of the alphabet gets a lively description in this engaging book.

Brown, M. W. (1994). *Four Fur Feet.* New York: Hyperion. The reader is drawn to the /f/ sound as the phrase "four fur feet" is repeated in every sentence.

Brown, M. W. (1989). *Goodnight Moon.* New York: Scholastic. A classic tale of a youngster who bids every conceivable object good night.

Bunting, E. (1991). *In the Haunted House.* New York: Clarion. A little girl and her father make some discoveries in a haunted house.

Butler, J., & Schade, S. (1990). *I Love You, Good Night.* New York: Simon and Schuster. In a sweet and rhythmic way, a mother and child tell each other good night.

Carter, D. (1990). *More Bugs in Boxes.* New York: Simon and Schuster. A pop-up book that presents a series of questions about make-believe bugs found inside a variety of boxes.

Chapman, C. (1993). *Pass the Fritters, Critters.* New York: Four Winds. Hungry animals discover a very important word.

Cole, J. (1989). *Anna Banana: 101 Jump-Rope Rhymes.* New York: Morrow. A collection of 101 jump-rope rhymes arranged by categories.

Cooper, M. (1997). *I Got a Family.* New York: Owlet. A young girl describes the members of her family and how they love her.

de Regniers, B.; Moore, E.; White, M.; & Carr, J. (1988). *Sing a Song of Popcorn.* New York: Scholastic. Several poems in this book draw children's attention to the patterns and rhythms of words. Filled with beautiful illustrations.

Degen, B. (1995). *Jamberry.* New York: Harper & Row. A little boy and a lovable bear have plenty of adventures in the fantastic world of Berryland.

Ehlert, L. (1989). *Eating the Alphabet.* San Diego: Harcourt Brace. Fruits and vegetables are offered for each letter of the alphabet.

Ehlert, L. (1993). *Nuts to You.* San Diego: Harcourt Brace. A squirrel had quite an adventure in an urban apartment.

Emberly, B. (1992). *One Wide River to Cross.* Boston: Little, Brown. Through the use of rhyme, the author describes the animals gathering on board Noah's Ark.

Fleming, D. (1991). *In the Tall, Tall Grass.* New York: Henry Holt & Company. Lots of rhyming text focuses on the creatures found in the grass all through the day.

Fleming, D. (1994). *Barnyard Banter.* New York: Henry Holt & Company. All the animals make their usual sounds, but where is the missing goose?

Florian, D. (1998). *The Beast Feast.* New York: Voyager. Different beasts are described in rhyming verses.

Fox, M. (1997). *Time for Bed.* San Diego: Harcourt Brace. Young animals, one by one, go to sleep in this rhyming bedtime story.

Galdone, P. (1984). *Henny Penny.* New York: Houghton Mifflin. Fun and silly rhyming highlight this classic tale about a dumbstruck chicken who believes the sky has fallen.

Ginsburg, M. (1987). *Across the Stream.* New York: Greenwillow. A gentle bedtime story designed to chase away bad dreams.

Gordon, J. (1991). *Six Sleepy Sheep.* New York: Puffin. Lots of fun uses for the letter *s* as six sheep try desperately to fall asleep.

Hague, K. (1984). *Alphabears.* New York: Henry Holt and Company. Twenty-six teddy bears introduce the alphabet through the use of alliteration.

Hague, M. (1999). *Michael Hague's Teddy Bear, Teddy Bear.* New York: Tupelo Books. The activities of a teddy bear are followed in this classic rhyme.

Hoberman, M. A. (2000). *Eency Weency Spider.* Boston: Little Brown. The Eency Weency Spider climbs the water spout and discovers some characters from Mother Goose.

Hoberman, M. A. (1982). *A House Is a House for Me.* New York: Puffin. The living quarters of a variety of animals are listed in rhyming fashion.

Hutchins, P. (1989). *Don't Forget the Bacon.* New York: Mulberry. A young boy brings back all the wrong items from the market.

Hutchins, P. (1989). *The Wind Blew.* New York: Aladdin. A cumulative tale in which the wind snatches objects everywhere. Lots of humor throughout.

Krauss, R. (1999). *I Can Fly.* New York: Golden Press. A variety of animals with sounds and actions that rhyme highlight this easy-to-read book.

Kuskin, K. (1990). *Roar and More.* New York: Harper & Row. Another book that focuses on the many different kinds of sounds that animals make.

Lewison, W. (1992). *Buzz Said the Bee.* New York: Scholastic. Animals climb over one another in order to get to the top of an animal pile. As they do, they perform some sort of rhyming action.

Lindbergh, R. (1990). *The Day the Goose Got Loose.* New York: Dial. A goose gets loose at the farm and everyone's in an uproar.

Martin, B., Jr. (1970). *Brown Bear, Brown Bear, What Do You See?* Orlando, Florida: Harcourt Brace and Company. A wonderful word play book—perfect for every classroom.

Martin, B., Jr., & Archambault, J. (1986). *Barn Dance!* New York: Holt, Rinehart and Winston. A sleepless boy hears the sound of music and follows it across the fields to a barn dance.

Martin, B., Jr., & Archambault, J. (1989). *Chicka, Chicka, Boom Boom.* New York: Simon and Schuster. The whole alphabet tries to climb a coconut tree in this delightful and engaging book for all your readers.

Martin, B., Jr., & Carle, E. (1991). *Polar Bear, Polar Bear, What Do You Hear?* New York: Henry Holt and Company. Various types of animals make distinctive types of sounds. Ideal for young children to imitate.

McPhail, D. (1993). *Pigs Aplenty, Pigs Galore.* New York: Dutton. A group of pigs invade a house and have a wonderful party.

Neitzel, S. (1994). *The Jacket I Wear in the Snow.* New York: Mulberry. All the clothes needed to play in the snow are named by a young girl.

Oppenheim, J. (1990). *Have You Seen Birds?* New York: Scholastic. A simple description of different types of birds, how they sound and what they do.

Oppenheim, J. (1997). *Not Now, Said the Cow.* New York: Gareth Stevens. Based on "The Little Red Hen," a crow asks his friends for help in planting corn.

Patz, N. (1989). *Moses Supposes the Toeses are Roses.* San Diego: Harcourt Brace. Rhyming, alliteration, and assonance make this collection of poems fun to read and fun to imitate.

Prelutsky, J. (1982). *The Baby Uggs are Hatching.* New York: Mulberry. Lots of language play and tons of silly imaginative words highlight this delightful collection of read-aloud poems.

Prelutsky, J. (1988). *Tyrannosaurus Was a Beast: Dinosaur Poems.* New York: Greenwillow. Lots of funny poems about all sorts of dinosaurs.

Raffi. (1987). *Down by the Bay.* New York: Crown. Two youngsters make up a collection of rhyming verses using various animals.

Raffi. (1989). *Tingalayo.* New York: Crown. Lots of rhyme and rhythm highlight this humorous book by a well-loved musician.

Sendak, M. (1991). *Alligators All Around.* New York: HarperTrophy. Lots of alliteration complement the letters of the alphabet as they are introduced by various animals.

Seuss, Dr. (1963). *Dr. Seuss's ABC.* New York: Random House. Each letter of the alphabet is presented along with an amusing sentence full of alliteration.

Seuss, Dr. (1965). *Fox in Socks.* New York: Random House. The fox tries to trip up the reader in this all-time favorite book.

Seuss, Dr. (1976). *One Fish Two Fish, Red Fish Blue Fish.* New York: Random House. A classic Dr. Seuss story—ideal for reading aloud.

Suess, Dr. (1974). *There's a Wocket in my Pocket.* New York: Random House. Lots of nonsense creatures are found around the house in this wonderful play on language.

Shaw, N. (1986). *Sheep in a Jeep.* Boston: Houghton Mifflin. The sheep go on another crazy adventure and get themselves into more trouble and more hilarious rhymes.

Shaw, N. (1989). *Sheep on a Ship.* Boston: Houghton Mifflin. Short verses and punchy language highlight this fun-to-read and fun-to-listen-to book.

Shaw, N. (1992). *Sheep Out to Eat.* Boston: Houghton Mifflin. A delightful entry in the *Sheep* series, guaranteed to please.

Sheppard, J. (1994). *Splash, Splash.* New York: Macmillan Publishing Company. A fun book to read aloud to any class.

Showers, P. (1993). *The Listening Walk.* New York: HarperTrophy. Phonemes predominate throughout this book as imaginative sounds are created for many types of everyday objects.

Silverstein, S. (1981). *A Giraffe and a Half.* New York: HarperCollins. Lots of cumulative and rhyming patterns in this story about a very unusual giraffe.

Speed, T. (1995). *Two Cool Cows.* New York: Putnam's. A modern rendition of "Hey Diddle Diddle" follows the adventures of two cool cows.

Staines, B. (1993). *All God's Critters Got a Place in the Choir.* New York: Puffin. All the creatures in the world have a place in the choir as well as lots of rhyming opportunities, too.

Van Allsburg, C. (1987). *The Z Was Zapped.* Boston: Houghton Mifflin. Letters of the alphabet get into a series of escalating mishaps until the final catastrophe of all.

Wells, R. (1973). *Noisy Nora.* New York: Dial. Nora makes more and more noise in order to get her parents' attention.

Westcott, N. B. (1998). *The Lady with the Alligator Purse.* Boston: Little, Brown. This classic jump-rope rhyme is full of nonsense.

Williams, S. (1969). *I Went Walking.* San Diego: Gulliver Books. Children will find this to be an engaging and delightful book.

Winthrop, E. (1988). *Shoes.* New York: Harper Trophy. Lots and lots of rhymes about shoes invite youngsters to create their own verses.

Wood, A. (1992). *Silly Sally.* San Diego: Harcourt Brace. Silly Sally makes lots of friends in this nonsensical book that's full of fun.

Yektai, N. (1991). *Bears in Pairs.* New York: Aladdin. Forty-eight bears, all in pairs, parade through the pages of this delightful read-aloud book.

Yolen, J. (1992). *Street Rhymes Around the World.* Honesdale, PA: Boyds Mills. Poems and poetry from around the world highlight this multicultural book.

Ziefert, H., & Brown, H. (1996). *What Rhymes with Eel?* New York: Viking. Lots of rhyming words and lots of rhyming pictures make this a fun book for every beginning reader.

Nursery Rhyme Activities

NURSERY RHYMES SHOULD BE a regular and consistent part of any phonemic awareness program. Not only do nursery rhymes introduce children to the rhythm and rhyme of language; so too do they provide youngsters with wonderful opportunities to engage in a wide variety of playful language activities. The daily use of nursery rhymes lets children know that language is full of fun and full of inventive and creative ways to manipulate language.

Nursery rhymes provide children (and their teachers) with a host of engaging activities that are light and engaging. Reading a familiar rhyme or turning a rhyme into a sing-along lets students know that the sounds of language can be shared in exciting and dynamic ways. To that end, nursery rhymes can be a daily part of classroom life beyond any formal phonemic awareness program.

This section contains a variety of nursery rhymes to share with your children. Accompanying each of the rhymes in this section are interactive activities that encourage children to expand and extend the rhyme. There is no particular order for the activities. Nor is it necessary for you to use all the activities for a rhyme. Feel free to pick and choose those rhymes and activities that will allow for the highest degree of language play in accordance with the needs, interests, and abilities of your students. Return to previously shared rhymes and activities throughout the course of your phonemic awareness program. Doing so will allow children to participate in favorite rhymes and activities.

It is strongly suggested that children spend lots of time with these rhymes since they may not have heard them at home. These rhymes are also useful as elements in other parts of your classroom literacy program. And, besides, they're just plain fun to share with children on a regular basis.

Humpty Dumpty

Humpty Dumpty
Sat on a wall.
Humpty Dumpty
Had a great fall.
All the king's horses
And all the king's men
Cannot put Humpty
Dumpty together again.

Activity: After children are familiar with this nursery rhyme, invite them to contribute their own rhymes. For example, say the first three lines and invite students to add a fourth line of their own choosing. ("Humpty Dumpty sat on a wall. Humpty Dumpty. . . . What sentence could we add to the end that would make this rhyme?")

Activity: Say the rhyme out loud to students. Say it again, replacing the last word in the second line with the name of a piece of furniture. Invite youngsters to contribute a new fourth line ending in a word that rhymes with the new word at the end of the second line. For example, "Humpty Dumpty sat on a chair. Humpty Dumpty. . . . (had lots of hair)" or "Humpty Dumpty sat on a bed. Humpty Dumpty. . . . (fell on his head)" or "Humpty Dumpty sat on a box. Humpty Dumpty. . . . (saw a red fox)."

Activity: Replace "Humpty Dumpty" with the names of children in the class and reread the rhyme out loud to students. For example "Michael Spikel sat on a wall. Michael Spikel had a great fall. . . ." Or "Donna Lonna sat on a wall. Donna Lonna had a great fall. . . ." Invite youngsters to contribute imaginative names for each person in the room. Invite students to repeat the rhyme along with you for each new name.

Hickory, Dickory, Dock

Hickory, dickory, dock,

The mouse ran up the clock.

The clock struck one,

The mouse ran down,

Hickory, dickory, dock.

Activity: After students are familiar with the rhyme, invite them to suggest letters (consonants preferred) in place of the beginning consonants for each of the first three words and last three words. Begin with identical consonants. For example: "Mickory, mickory, mock." When students are comfortable with identical consonants, move on to random consonants. For example: "Tickory, gickory, gock. . . ." Or "Mickory, bickory, bock. . . ."

Activity: Invite students to substitute a new consonant sound in the middle of each of the first three words and last three words in the rhyme. For example: "Himmory, dimmory, domm . . ." or "Hittory, dittory, dott. . . ."

Activity: Encourage students to suggest new alliterative letters for each of the first three words and last three words of the rhyme. For example: "Hickory, hickory, hock . . ." or "Sickory, sickory, sock. . . ."

Activity: For lots of silliness (and just plain fun), invite youngsters to suggest new rhyming sentences for each pair of numbers. For example: One, two, eat some stew; Three, four, daddy can snore; Five, six, my dog eats sticks; Seven, eight, my nose is straight; Nine, ten, let's do it again. You may want to post some of these silly sentences on a classroom bulletin board.

Activity: Say each even number separately along with two rhyming words. Invite children to suggest one more rhyming word for each number. For example:

Two: shoe, blue, _____

Four: door, more, _____

Six: mix, tricks, _____

Eight: straight, late, _____

Ten: pen, Ken, _____

One, Two, Buckle My Shoe

One, two, buckle my shoe

Three, four, shut the door

Five, six, pick up sticks

Seven, eight, lay them straight

Nine, ten, the big fat hen.

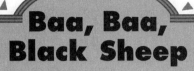

Baa, Baa, Black Sheep

Baa, Baa, black sheep,

Have you any wool?

Yes, sir, yes, sir,

Three bags full:

One for the master,

One for the dame,

And one for the little boy

Who lives down the lane.

Activity: Repeat the first four lines of the rhyme and invite students to clap once after you say each word. Repeat several times. Change the first four lines to the following two rhymes, and invite children to repeat the activity by clapping once after each word.

Oink, oink, black pig
Have you any pork?
Yes, sir, yes, sir,
In a bag with a cork.

Quack, quack, black duck
Do you like to drink?
Yes, sir, yes, sir,
From the cup that is pink.

Invite children to note that each word resulted in a single clap (each word had one part or syllable).

Activity: After reading the rhyme several times, use a classroom puppet to say each of the following words in parts. Invite children to listen carefully and say each word as a whole:

/y/ /e/ /s/ (yes)
/b/ /a/ /g/ /s/ (bags)
/d/ /a/ /m/ (dam)
/b/ /oy/ (boy)
/l/ /a/ /n/ (lane)

Three Blind Mice

Three blind mice, three blind mice;
See how they run, see how they run!
They all ran after the farmer's wife,
Who cut off their tails with a carving knife.
Have you ever seen such a sight
In your life as three blind mice?

Activity: After children are familiar with this rhyme, tell them that you are going to make some silly changes to lines 1 and 2. Tell them that you will say a line with a new word at the end and they must repeat it after you. For example, you say, "Three blind dice, three blind dice," and the children repeat, "Three blind dice, three blind dice." Following are substitute words you can use for line 1 and for line 2:

Line 1: dice, lice, rice, price, slice, spice
Line 2: bun, fun, nun, pun, run, sun

Activity: Say one of the following word pairs to students. Tell children that the first word in each pair is a word from the rhyme and that the second word in each pair is a word that you added. Invite students to suggest a third word that rhymes with the first two:

three–tree _____   run–fun _____

blind–mind _____   ran–fan _____

mice–rice _____   cut–nut _____

see–me _____   seen–mean _____

they–play _____   life–knife _____

Rub-a-Dub-Dub

Rub-a-dub-dub,

Three men in a tub,

And how do you think they got there?

The butcher, the baker,

The candlestick maker,

They all jumped out of a rotten potato,

'Twas enough to make a man stare.

Activity: After children are familiar with this rhyme, tell them that you are going to change the first two lines. Tell the students that you will make up some nonsense words for the first line and they must make up a rhyming nonsense word for the second line. For example, you say, "mub-a-mub-mub," and the children respond, "three men in a sub." Keep this activity light and full of nonsense for maximum results.

Activity: Create a chant with children using selected words from the rhyme. For example:

It begins with /r/
And ends with /ub/.
Put them together
And they say _____ (rub).

Invite children to blend the sounds together and chorus the correct answer. Repeat the chant several times using some of the following words from the rhyme:

dub: /d/ /ub/
three: /th/ /ree/
tub: /t/ /ub/
think: /th/ /ink/
they: /th/ /ey/
there: /th/ /ere/

Activity: Repeat this rhyme several times, each time changing the letter at the end of line 6 to each of the following:

C   D   E   G   P   T   V   Z

Invite children to repeat the sixth line each time you substitute a new letter.

Activity: Repeat the activity above and change the letter at the end of line 6 to each of the following letters. Each time, complete the last two lines of the rhyme and invite children to suggest an appropriate rhyming word. For example:

A (kay, may)
I (sly, pie, rye)
O (flow, crow, moe)
U (you, lou, crew)

Activity: Repeat the rhyme for children, each time altering the first two lines of the rhyme. Substitute the following words:

Fat-a-cake, fat-a-cake, baker's pan
Mat-a-cake, mat-a-cake, baker's tan
Bat-a-cake, bat-a-cake, baker's fan
Cat-a-cake, cat-a-cake, baker's ran
Hat-a-cake, hat-a-cake, baker's can

Pat-a-Cake

Pat-a-cake, pat-a-cake,
Baker's man!
Bake me a cake,
As fast as you can.
Pat it, and prick it,
And mark it with a B.
Put it in the oven
For Baby and me.

Little Jack Horner

Little Jack Horner

Sat in a corner

Eating his Christmas pie;

He put in his thumb,

And pulled out a plum,

And cried, "What a good

boy am I!"

Activity: After the children have heard this rhyme several times, say each sentence individually. Choose one word in each sentence to read in sound segments instead of as a whole word. Invite children to orally blend the sounds in the target word and say it aloud.

Little /J/ /a/ /k/ Horner
 (What was his name?)
/S/ /a/ /t/ in a corner
 (What did he do?)
Eating /h/ /i/ /s/ Christmas pie;
 (Whose pie?)
He /p/ /u/ /t/ in his thumb
 (What did he do?)
And pulled out a /p/ /l/ /u/ /m/,
 (What did he pull out?)
And cried, "What a /g/ /oo/ /d/ boy am I!"
 (What kind of boy was he?)

Activity: Repeat the first five lines of the rhyme for your students, but change the body part at the end of line 4 (see samples below). Invite the children to suggest a rhyming word for the end of line 5. For example:

Hand: band, land
Nose: rose, toes
Head: bread, sled
Ear: tear, gear
Leg: peg, keg
Arm: farm, charm

Little Miss Muffet

Little Miss Muffet
Sat on a tuffet,
Eating her curds and whey.
There came a big spider,
Who sat down beside her,
And frightened Miss Muffet away.

Activity: After children are familiar with this rhyme, ask them to listen to the following words: *muffet, sat, tuffet*. Point out that all three of these words end in the same sound (/t/). Tell students that you want them to listen to the following words from the rhyme and tell you the sound at the end of each word.

miss /s/   came /m/
on /n/   big /g/
her /r/   spider /r/
whey /a/   beside /d/

Activity: Tell the children that you are going to say three words, one word from the rhyme plus two other words. You want them to listen closely and tell you the sound they hear that is the same in all three words. For example, in the first set below, you would say "miss, mars, map." The children would respond with "/m/." (Note that the target sound is in the same position—initial, medial, final—in all three words in a set.)

miss, mars, map (/m/)
sat, soup, soap (/s/)
her, cheer, car (/r/)
and, road, word (/d/)
came, pain, late (/a/)
down, can, nine (/n/)

To Market

To market, to market, to buy a fat pig,
Home again, home again, jiggety-jig.
To market, to market, to buy a fat hog,
Home again, home again, jiggety-jog.

Activity: Repeat the rhyme several times. Then say the first line again, substituting one of the words from the list below. Invite children to say the second line, substituting the last word with an appropriate rhyming word.

cat	shark	dog	horse	duck
bear	fly	mouse	whale	deer

For example:

You say, "To market, to market, to buy a fat cat."
Children say, "Home again, home again, jiggety-jat."

Activity: After students are familiar with the rhyme, tell them that you will say it again, but this time you will change the first line to "To barket, to barket, to buy a fat pig." To illustrate this, write the word market on the chalkboard, erase the letter *m*, and replace it with the letter *b*. Pronounce the nonsense word formed. Say the line again and invite the children to repeat after you. Afterward, change the word market to each of the following nonsense words and invite children to repeat the line after you each time: *barket, darket, harket, jarket, narket, parket.*

Activity: Repeat the rhyme several times, each time saying the second line with a substituted consonant (see below) for the *j* in the original version. Invite the children to repeat after you each time. For example: "To market, to market, to buy a fat pig, Home again, home again, tiggety-tig."

B: biggety-big	M: miggety-mig	T: tiggety-tig
D: diggety-dig	P: piggety-pig	W: wiggety-wig
F: figgety-fig	R: riggety-rig	
L: liggety-lig	S: siggety-sig	

One for the Money

One for the money,
And two for the show,
Three to get ready,
And four to go.

Activity: Using words from the rhyme, ask the children each of the following questions:

What rhymes with *one* and begins with /f/? (*fun*)

What rhymes with *money* and begins with /h/? (*honey*)

What rhymes with *two* and begins with /m/? (*moo*)

What rhymes with *show* and begins with /b/? (*bow, blow*)

What rhymes with *three* and begins with /m/? (*me*)

What rhymes with *get* and begins with /p/? (*pet*)

What rhymes with *four* and begins with /m/? (*more*)

What rhymes with *go* and begins with /n/? (*no*)

Activity: Provide the children with a fun way to delete sounds from words with this activity. Say the following sentences, each of which uses a word from the rhyme. For each word invite the children to delete the appropriate sound. Point out that some of their responses may be nonsense words.

Say *for* without the /f/.

Say *two* without the /t/.

Say *show* without the /sh/.

Say *three* without the /th/.

Say *get* without the /g/.

Say *to* without the /t/.

Say *go* without the /g/.

Say *money* without the /e/.

Say *and* without the /d/.

Say *show* without the /o/.

Say *get* without the /t/.

Say *ready* without the /e/.

Say *four* without the /r/.

Pease Porridge Hot

Pease porridge hot,

Pease porridge cold,

Pease porridge in the pot

Nine days old.

Some like it hot,

Some like it cold,

Some like it in the pot,

Nine days old!

Activity: After the children have had sufficient oral practice with this rhyme, print the first four lines on the chalkboard. Tell the children that you are going to do something silly and erase the first letter from some of the words (see below). Read the new lines to the children and invite them to repeat them back to you. Repeat this activity several times.

_ease _orridge _ot,
_ease _orridge _old,
_ease _orridge in the _ot
_ine _ays _old.

After the children are used to the pattern, tell them that you are going to add a new letter to each of the words from which you subtracted letters before. Say the new lines (as in the sample below) and invite the children to repeat after you.

Target Letters: R M Z S K B
Sample: Rease, rorridge rot,
Rease rorridge rold,
Rease rorridge in the rot
Rine rays rold.

Activity: Tell the students that you are going to say two parts of a word from the rhyme. Invite them to put the two parts together to make a word.

/p/ and _ease_   /p/ and _ot_
/h/ and _ot_   /n/ and _ine_
/c/ and _old_   /s/ and _ome_
/l/ and _ike_

Activity: Tell the students that you are going to say two words together—one word from the rhyme plus one additional word. Invite the children to each put two thumbs up if the two words rhyme.

sing–ring	when–that
song–long	birds–ducks
pocket–rocket	to–moo
rye–dog	dish–fish
four–sand	set–more
pie–tie	king–sing

Activity: Tell the children that you are going to ask them some riddles using words from the rhyme. Invite them to figure out the answer for each riddle.

What rhymes with /ing/ and begins with /s/? (*sing*)
What rhymes with /ong/ and begins with /s/? (*song*)
What rhymes with /ull/ and begins with /f/? (*full*)
What rhymes with /or/ and begins with /f/? (*four*)
What rhymes with /i/ and begins with /p/? (*pie*)
What rhymes with /irds/ and begins with /b/? (*birds*)
What rhymes with /ish/ and begins with /d/? (*dish*)
What rhymes with /et/ and begins with /s/? (*set*)
What rhymes with /ing/ and begins with /k/? (*king*)

Activity: After the children have heard the rhyme several times, invite them to listen to the following word parts. Invite the students to put the word parts together to form a word used in the rhyme.

six–pence	o–pen	pock–et	be–gan
twen–ty	dain–ty	black–birds	be–fore

Sing a Song of Sixpence

Sing a song of sixpence,
A pocket full of rye;
Four-and-twenty blackbirds
Baked in a pie!
When the pie was opened,
The birds began to sing!
Wasn't that a dainty dish
To set before the king?

There Was an Old Woman

There was an old woman
Who lived in a shoe.
She had so many children,
She didn't know what to do.
She gave them some broth
Without any bread.
She kissed them all sweetly
And sent them to bed.

Activity: After the children are familiar with this rhyme, tell them that you will say the first two lines of the rhyme to them, but you will change the word at the end of line 2. You'll then say the third line and the first word of the fourth line—inviting them to complete the fourth line with something that will rhyme with the new word inserted into line 2. You may wish to share the two examples below:

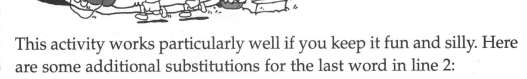

There was an old woman
Who lived in a *hat*
She had so many children
She became very *fat*.

There was an old woman
Who lived in a *car*
She had so many children
She couldn't drive *far*.

This activity works particularly well if you keep it fun and silly. Here are some additional substitutions for the last word in line 2:

    sock   shirt   dress   box   train   store   tree

Activity: Tell the children that you are going to say some words from the rhyme. Invite them to tell you the number of sounds they here in each word.

/w/ /a/ /s/	/g/ /a/ /v/
/i/ /n/	/s/ /o/ /m/
/h/ /a/ /d/	/a/ /ll/
/s/ /o/	/b/ /e/ /d/
/t/ /o/	/d/ /o/

Old King Cole

Old King Cole
Was a merry old soul,
And a merry old soul was he.
He called for his pipe,
And he called for his bowl,
And he called for his fiddlers three.

Activity: Tell the children that you will say three words aloud to them. Invite them to tell you the word in each group that does not rhyme with the other two.

old, bold, pipe	cup, merry, berry
Cole, mom, bowl	for, more, nine
he, three, phone	light, king, sing

Activity: Tell the students that you are going to repeat some of the words from the rhyme. Invite them to listen carefully and tell you the middle sound in each word. Use the following words. (Say each word in a stretched pronunciation—for example: C-ooooooooo-le.)

Cole (/o/)	his (/i/)
old (/l/)	pipe (/i/)
merry (/r/)	bowl (/o/)
and (/n/)	was (/a/)

The Cat and the Fiddle

Hey, diddle, diddle,

The cat and the fiddle,

The cow jumped

Over the moon.

The little dog laughed

To see such sport,

And the dish ran away

With the spoon.

Activity: Repeat the first two lines several times. Write the word *diddle* in large letters on the chalkboard. Tell the children that you are going to replace the first letter in that word with another letter. Say the new word for them and then invite them to repeat the first two lines using the new word. You may wish to use the following words, and then let the children invent their own:

biddle	middle	viddle
hiddle	niddle	widdle
jiddle	riddle	yiddle
kiddle	siddle	ziddle
liddle	tiddle	

Activity: Tell the students that you are going to create some silly sentences using words from the rhyme. Tell them that each word in a sentence will start with the same sound. After you've read each sentence to the class, invite the students to tell you the beginning sound for each word in that sentence. Here are some silly sentences to read:

Cute cats cut cartoons.
Four fat fiddles fight.
Crazy cows can creep.
Just Jack jumped.
Mary made marshmallow moons.
Dogs dream daily.
Seven sailors see Sam.
Randy ran rapidly.

Activity: After children are familiar with this rhyme, say the first line for them and ask them to respond with the second line. Then change the word at the end of the first line and invite the children to respond with the second line. Repeat several times, each time replacing the word at the end of line 1 with one of the words below, and then saying the line aloud for children to be followed by the children responding with line 2 (tell children that some of these words are nonsense words).

car	bar	tar	far	lar
mar	var	gar	par	sar

Activity: Repeat the activity above using lines 3 and 4 in the rhyme. Each time, substitute the word at the end of line 3 with one of the following words (again, some words will be nonsense words).

bye	lie	my	vie	kie	tie
sigh	die	rye	gie	pie

Twinkle, Twinkle, Little Star

Twinkle, twinkle, little star,

How I wonder what you are,

Up above the world so high,

Like a diamond in the sky.

Twinkle, twinkle, little star,

How I wonder what you are!

SonG aNd DraMa ActiVitiEs

THE RHYMES AND RHYTHMS of language can be playfully shared with children by incorporating songs and drama activities into your everyday activities. Songs are playful ways for children to learn about and utilize language in a variety of activities and sharing opportunities. They are wonderful ways to open up the school day, delightful introductions to lessons and specific learning activities, and creative ventures into using language across the curriculum.

Use the following songs and their attendant activities as part of your daily lessons in phonemic awareness. As with all of the activities in this book, the emphasis is on fun. Let children know that songs are simply playful interpretations of the language we use every day. In addition, they are delightful opportunities for groups of people to share and participate in the sounds of language.

Plan to incorporate a song or two in your daily interactions with children. Your ability to sing (or lack thereof) should not influence the use of songs and the accompanying activities. By modeling the fun you have in singing songs, children will sense the enjoyment they can experience through song and drama activities. Singing can be one of the most anticipated portions of any phonemic awareness program and certainly one that can be done at any time during the school day.

Row, Row, Row Your Boat

Row, row, row your boat
Gently down the stream.
Merrily, merrily, merrily, merrily,
Life is but a dream.

Write the song on a sheet of chart paper or the chalkboard. Invite children to sing the song with you several times. Tell children that you will sing the song alone, but this time you will change the line "Merrily, merrily, merrily, merrily" to "Perrily, perrily, perrily, perrily." To illustrate this, write the word *merrily* on the chalkboard in large letters. Erase the letter *m* and replace it with the letter *p*. This will demonstrate to children that when a letter is removed and replaced with another letter, a new word is created. Pronounce the nonsense word created. Continue singing the song, each time changing the first letter in the word *merrily* to create a new third line. Here are some other possibilities: *terrily, berrily, serrily, zerrily, rerrily.* After you have done this several times, invite children to join with you in singing the song with a nonsense word for the third line.

Old MacDonald Had a Farm

Old MacDonald had a farm, E–I–E–I–O.

And on this farm he had a pig, E–I–E–I–O.

With a pig, pig here,

And a pig, pig there,

Here a pig, there a pig,

Everywhere a pig–pig.

Old MacDonald had a farm, E–I–E–I–O.

Write the song on a sheet of chart paper. Explain to children that you are going to teach them a different version of the song. In the new version, the names of the children in the room are on the farm. Track the print as you sing. Sing the song several times, each time substituting a letter sound *and* the name of a child in the room that begins with that sound into the song. After you create each new verse, invite youngsters to sing along with you. For example:

Old MacDonald had a farm, E–I–E–I–O.
And on this farm he had a /t/, E–I–E–I–O.
With a *Tom*, *Tom* here
And a *Tom*, *Tom* there,
Here a *Tom*, there a *Tom*,
Everywhere a *Tom*–*Tom*.
Old MacDonald had a farm, E–I–E–I–O.

or

Old MacDonald had a farm, E–I–E–I–O.
And on this farm he had a /k/, E–I–E–I–O.
With a *Katie*, *Katie* here
And a *Katie*, *Katie* there,
Here a *Katie*, there a *Katie*,
Everywhere a *Katie*–*Katie*.
Old MacDonald had a farm, E–I–E–I–O.

Pop! Goes the Weasel

All around the mulberry bush

The monkey chased the weasel.

The monkey thought 'twas all in fun.

Pop! Goes the weasel.

A penny for a spool of thread,

A penny for a needle.

That's the way the money goes.

Pop! Goes the weasel.

Print the song on the chalk-board (if desired, print the word *Pop* in oversized letters). Teach the children the tune and invite them to sing it with you several times (place an extra emphasis on the word *Pop*). After they are familiar with the pace and rhythm of the song, tell the children that you are going to change one of the words. Erase the first *P* in the word *pop*. Replace that letter with one of the letters or letter combinations below:

H   M   T   CH   DR   SH   ST

After each replacement, invite the children to sing the song again and, as before, to place an extra emphasis on the *_op* word. Afterward, take time to discuss how each of the new words rhymed with all of its replacements.

This Old Man

This old man, he played one,
He played knick knack with his thumb,
With a knick knack, paddy whack,
Give the dog a bone;
This old man came rolling home.

This old man, he played two,
He played knick knack with my shoe,
With a knick knack, paddy whack,
Give the dog a bone;
This old man came rolling home.

This old man, he played three,
He played knick knack on my knee,
With a knick knack, paddy whack,
Give the dog a bone;
This old man came rolling home.

This old man, he played four,
He played knick knack at my door,
With a knick knack, paddy whack,
Give the dog a bone;
This old man came rolling home.

This old man, he played five,
He played knick knack, jazz and jive,
With a knick knack, paddy whack,
Give the dog a bone;
This old man came rolling home.

This old man, he played six,
He played knick knack with his sticks,
With a knick knack, paddy whack,
Give the dog a bone;
This old man came rolling home.

This old man, he played seven,
He played knick knack with his pen,
With a knick knack, paddy whack,
Give the dog a bone;
This old man came rolling home.

This old man, he played eight,
He played knick knack on my gate,
With a knick knack, paddy whack,
Give the dog a bone;
This old man came rolling home.

This old man, he played nine,
He played knick knack, rise and shine,
With a knick knack, paddy whack,
Give the dog a bone;
This old man came rolling home.

This old man, he played ten,
He played knick knack in my den,
With a knick knack, paddy whack,
Give the dog a bone;
This old man came rolling home.

Make up two sets of ten flashcards. On the first set of cards, print one number from 1 to 10 on one side of the card. On the reverse side of each card, print the word for the number in capital letters. On the second set of cards, draw or glue pictures of the items mentioned at the end of line 2 in each stanza. On the reverse of each card, print the name of the object as in the song. The cards will look as follows:

1	one		thumb
2	two		shoe
3	three		knee
4	four		door
5	five		jive
6	six		sticks
7	seven		pen
8	eight		gate
9	nine		shine
10	ten		den

After you and the children have sung the song through once, tell them that you will be making some changes. Sing the song through several times, using the flashcards as illustrated on the previous page:

1. Sing the song and hold up the appropriate number card for each number at the end of line 1 in each stanza.

2. Sing the song and hold up the number word card for each number.

3. Sing the song and hold up the picture card for each item at the end of the second line in each stanza.

4. Sing the song and hold up the word card for each item.

5. Sing the song and hold up both the number card and picture card for the appropriate items in each stanza.

6. Sing the song and hold up both the number word card and the picture word card for the appropriate items in each stanza.

After children are comfortable and familiar with the song, invite them to help you match the number cards with their corresponding picture cards in a pocket chart. Place the word *one* in one side of the chart and ask children to place the corresponding rhyming picture card (*thumb*) on the other side of the chart. Go through all the numbers and all the rhyming words in this manner. If appropriate, provide children with the opportunity to mix and match the cards (using number cards with picture cards and word cards, for example).

Variation: This song is an all-time favorite because there are plenty of opportunities for children to get physically involved too. While singing the song, invite children to point to the item mentioned at the end of the second line in each stanza. If the item is difficult to point to (for example, *jive*), invite youngsters to create a special movement or dance that illustrates that "item."

Ring Around the Rosie

Ring around the rosie,

A pocket full of posies,

Ashes! Ashes!

We all fall down!

Write each of the lines of the song on a separate sentence strip. Place each of the sentence strips in a pocket chart. Using index cards, make up the word cards shown below.

Sing the song through with the children, pointing to each of the words as you sing them together. Then tell them that you will be changing the first word in the song. Take one of the word cards and place it in the pocket chart so that it covers the first word. Tell the children what the word is and then invite them to sing the song again using the new word in place of the original. Repeat this process several times using additional word cards to replace the word *ring*. Afterward, take some time to discuss with children how all of the word cards rhymed with the first word in the song.

king	sling
ring	sting
sing	swing
wing	thing
bring	spring
cling	string

Variation: This song is especially fun if you invite all the children to form a circle holding hands. As you sing the song, invite children to move together in a counterclockwise motion. When you get to the last line in the song, everybody (including you) should physically fall to the floor. After much laughter, everyone stands up again and sings a new version (with a new first word), again moving in a circle and falling down at the appropriate time.

The Ants Go Marching

The ants go marching one by one.
Hurrah! Hurrah!
The ants go marching one by one.
Hurrah! Hurrah!
The ants go marching one by one;
The little one stops to suck his thumb,
And they all go marching
Down
Into the ground
To get out
Of the rain.
Boom, boom, boom!

The ants go marching two by two.
Hurrah! Hurrah!
The ants go marching two by two.
Hurrah! Hurrah!
The ants go marching two by two;
The little one stops to tie his shoe,
And they all go marching
Down
Into the ground
To get out
Of the rain.
Boom, boom, boom!

The ants go marching three by three.
Hurrah! Hurrah!
The ants go marching three by three.
Hurrah! Hurrah!
The ants go marching three by three;
The little one stops to ride a bee,

And they all go marching
Down
Into the ground
To get out
Of the rain.
Boom, boom, boom!

The ants go marching four by four.
Hurrah! Hurrah!
The ants go marching four by four.
Hurrah! Hurrah!
The ants go marching four by four;
The little one stops to ask for more,
And they all go marching
Down
Into the ground
To get out
Of the rain.
Boom, boom, boom!

The ants go marching five by five.
Hurrah! Hurrah!
The ants go marching five by five.
Hurrah! Hurrah!
The ants go marching five by five;
The little one stops to jump and dive,
And they all go marching
Down
Into the ground
To get out
Of the rain.
Boom, boom, boom!

The ants go marching six by six.
Hurrah! Hurrah!
The ants go marching six by six.
Hurrah! Hurrah!
The ants go marching six by six;
The little one stops to pick up sticks,
And they all go marching
Down
Into the ground
To get out
Of the rain.
Boom, boom, boom!

The ants go marching seven by seven.
Hurrah! Hurrah!
The ants go marching seven by seven.
Hurrah! Hurrah!
The ants go marching seven by seven;
The little one stops to write with a pen,
And they all go marching
Down
Into the ground
To get out
Of the rain.
Boom, boom, boom!

The ants go marching eight by eight.
Hurrah! Hurrah!
The ants go marching eight by eight.
Hurrah! Hurrah!
The ants go marching eight by eight;
The little one stops to roller skate,

And they all go marching
Down
Into the ground
To get out
Of the rain.
Boom, boom, boom!

The ants go marching nine by nine.
Hurrah! Hurrah!
The ants go marching nine by nine.
Hurrah! Hurrah!
The ants go marching nine by nine;
The little one stops to drink and dine,
And they all go marching
Down
Into the ground
To get out
Of the rain.
Boom, boom, boom!

The ants go marching ten by ten.
Hurrah! Hurrah!
The ants go marching ten by ten.
Hurrah! Hurrah!
The ants go marching ten by ten;
The little one stops to shout
"THE END!"

Print the song on large sheets of newsprint or on chart paper. Teach the song to the students while pointing to the words as you sing them together. Invite the class to re-sing the entire song, except in this version you will be the only one to say the fifth line in each stanza (you and the children will all sing the other lines together). Tell the children that you will make up a new line for that part of the song. The line you create will have a word at the end that will rhyme with the number in that stanza. Here are some possibilities that you may wish to insert into this new version of the song:

One: The little one stops to have some fun.
The little one stops to chew some gum.

Two: The little one stops to eat some stew.
The little one stops to look at you.

Three: The little one stops to scratch a flea.
The little one stops to climb a tree.

Four: The little one stops to sleep and snore.
The little one stops to close the door.

Five: The little one stops to see a hive.
The little one stops to learn to drive.

Six: The little one stops to do some tricks.
The little one stops to look at ticks.

Seven: The little one stops in a lion's den.
The little one stops to pet a hen.

Eight: The little one stops to close the gate.
The little one stops to lick his plate.

Nine: The little one stops to read a sign.
The little one stops to say, "I'm fine!"

Variations:

• This song is a great way for young children to learn numbers and sequencing. I like to sing the song with children, each time having the requisite number of students come to the front of the room and simulate marching as the song is being sung. For example, for "The ants go marching one by one," one student stands in front of the others and marches in place during the singing of that verse; for "The ants go marching two by two," two students get up and "march" in front of the class as that verse is being sung. This continues throughout the song until the very end, when all students jump to their feet and shout, "THE END!"

• Invite students to beat their fists on a desk or the floor each time the "Boom, boom, boom" is sung. Children may also wish to stamp their feet during this part of the song.

It's Raining, It's Pouring

It's raining, it's pouring;

The old man is snoring.

He went to bed

And bumped his head

And couldn't get up in the morning

Print each line of the song on a strip of oaktag or cardboard for placement in a pocket chart. Print several extra sentence strips for lines 3 and 4 using the examples below. After the children are familiar with the rhyme and rhythm of the song, replace the sentence strips for lines 3 and 4 with those below and sing the song again with the children. Replace the strips in the pocket chart several times. Take time to inform children that the words at the end of sentence strip 3 and sentence strip 4 are rhyming words. As children become comfortable with this, they may wish to suggest their own pairs of rhyming words. You can print their suggestions on additional sentence strips and use them in singing the song.

He bumped his nose
On a pile of clothes

He bumped his back
On a big brown sack

He bumped his chin
On a big fat pin

He bumped his ring
On a piece of string

He bumped his brain
On a speedy train

He bumped his seat
On a pile of wheat

He bumped his feet
On a chocolate sweet

He bumped his throat
On a billy goat

He bumped his hip
On a potato chip

GRAMPS

A Tisket, A Tasket

A tisket, a tasket,
A green and yellow basket,
I wrote a letter to my love,
And on the way, I dropped it.

I dropped it, I dropped it,
And on the way, I dropped it.
A little boy picked it up
And put it in his pocket.

Print the song on a large sheet of newsprint. Sing it with the children several times until they are comfortable with the rhyme and rhythm of the song. Print the first line of the song on the chalkboard in large letters. Tell children that you will be making a change in two of the words in that line. Use the letter cards (see pages 176–183) one at a time to cover the first *t* in *tisket* and the *t* in *tasket*.

- For the first go-round, use multiple copies of the designated letter to cover up the two *t*s (for example, use two *d*s, two *f*s, or two *m*s).

- For the second go-round, use two different letters to replace the *t*s in *tisket* and *tasket* (for example, a *p* and an *s* or a *j* and a *k*).

Select from the following letters:

B	D	F	G	H	J	K	L
M	N	P	R	S	V	W	Z

Skip to My Lou

Skip, skip, skip to my Lou,

Skip, skip, skip to my Lou,

Skip, skip, skip to my Lou,

Skip to my Lou, my darlin'.

Fly's in the buttermilk, shoo, shoo, shoo,

Fly's in the buttermilk, shoo, shoo, shoo,

Fly's in the buttermilk, shoo, shoo, shoo,

Skip to my Lou, my darlin'.

Write the song on the chalkboard or a sheet of newsprint. Invite the children to sing the song with you several times. Then tell the children that you will be making some changes to some of the words. Erase the word *Lou* each time it occurs in the first stanza and erase the word *shoo* each time it occurs in the second stanza. Replace these words with word cards (taped to the board) selected from the pairs below. Sing the song each time. Afterward, point out to the children how the word pairs rhyme.

Jack–back	jail–sail	ring–king	fig–wig
dad–mad	rain–pain	hip–dip	boat–goat
bag–wag	game–lame	sock–rock	cold–sold
bed–red	gate–plate	duck–chuck	nose–close
bell–well	bride–hide	hole–mole	fly–cry
tick–lick	dime–time	bone–cone	

For example:

Skip, skip, skip to my fig,
Skip, skip, skip to my fig,
Skip, skip, skip to my fig,
Skip to my fig, my darlin'.

Fly's in the buttermilk, wig, wig, wig
Fly's in the buttermilk, wig, wig, wig,
Fly's in the buttermilk, wig, wig, wig,
Skip to my fig, my darlin'.

Variation: Invite children to form a circle. As they sing the song, they can skip together in a counterclockwise pattern for the first stanza. Then, for the second stanza, they can reverse their direction and skip in a clockwise motion.

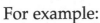

Oh, Dear, What Can the Matter Be?

Oh, dear, what can the matter be?
Oh, dear, what can the matter be?
Oh, dear, what can the matter be?
Johnny's so long at the fair.

He promised to buy me a bunch of blue ribbons;
He promised to buy me a bunch of blue ribbons;
He promised to buy me a bunch of blue ribbons;
To bind up my bonny brown hair.

And it's, oh, dear! What can the matter be?
Oh, dear, what can the matter be?
Oh, dear, what can the matter be?
Johnny's so long at the fair.

Print the song on a sheet of oaktag or newsprint. Write the last word in each of the three stanzas in extra-large letters. Tell the children that when they sing the song, you would like to have them emphasize (or shout) those words each time. Point out to the children that those three words all rhyme.

Make up several word cards using blank index cards. Use the words below. Tape one of the cards over the word *hair*. Invite the students to sing the song using the new word (again, they should emphasize—or shout—the new word just as they did for the other ending words). Plan time to discuss with children the fact that all of the new words still rhyme.

bear   stair   mare   pear   spare   chair

Variation: Invite the entire class to sing the song together, but designate one person to say the last word in each stanza alone (the class stops singing just before the last word in each stanza). Use the new words above and rotate this "assignment" among several different students.

Yankee Doodle

Yankee Doodle came to town,
A-ridin' on a pony;
Stuck a feather in his hat
And called it macaroni.

Yankee Doodle keep it up,
Yankee Doodle dandy,
Mind the music and the steps
And with the girls be handy.

Print the song on the chalkboard or on a sheet of newsprint. Teach this old-time favorite to your students. Then, substitute the name with the name of one of the children in the class for "Yankee Doodle" (it may be necessary to modify or alter names somewhat in order to get the necessary four-syllable count). Invite the class to sing the song using the name of a classmate. Continue the process using the names of as many students in the class as possible. For example:

Lauren Lauren came to town,
A-ridin' on a pony;
Stuck a feather in her hat
And called it macaroni.

or

Tyrone Simpson came to town
A-ridin' on a pony;
Stuck a feather in his hat
And called it macaroni.

Bibliography

Aliki. (1996). *Go Tell Aunt Rhody.* New York: Aladdin.

Birdseye, T. (1994). *She'll Be Comin' 'Round the Mountain.* New York: Holiday House.

Brown, M. (1993). *Hand Rhymes.* New York: Puffin.

Cole, J. (1989). *Anna Banana: 101 Jump-Rope Rhymes.* New York: Morrow.

Delacre, L. (1992). *Arroz con Leche: Popular Songs and Rhymes from Latin America.* New York: Scholastic.

Dunn, S. (1987). *Butterscotch Dreams.* Portsmouth, NH: Heinemann.

Hague, M. (1999). *Michael Hague's Teddy Bear, Teddy Bear.* New York: Tupelo Books.

Hart, J. (1982). *Singing Bee! A Collection of Favorite Children's Songs.* New York: Lothrop.

Hoberman, M. A. (1998). *Miss Mary Mack.* Boston: Little, Brown.

Jones, C. (1998). *This Old Man.* New York: Walter Lorraine.

Langstaff, J. (1991). *Oh, A-Hunting We Will Go.* New York: Aladdin.

Medearis, A. (1997). *The Zebra-Riding Cowboy: Folk Songs from the Old West.* New York: Owlet.

Oppenheim, J. (1991). *Eency Weency Spider.* New York: Bantam.

Peek, M. (1998). *Mary Wore Her Red Dress.* New York: Clarion.

Raffi. (1997). *Baby Beluga.* New York: Crown.

Raffi. (1999). *Down by the Bay.* New York: Crown.

Raffi. (1990). *Shake My Sillies Out.* New York: Crown.

Raffi. (1990). *The Wheels on the Bus.* New York: Crown.

Schwartz, A. (1999). *And the Green Grass Grew All Around: Folk Poetry from Everyone.* New York: HarperCollins.

Weiss, N. (1987). *If You're Happy and You Know It.* New York: Greenwillow.

Westcott, N. (1988). *I Know an Old Lady Who Swallowed a Fly.* Boston: Little, Brown.

Westcott, N. (1992). *Peanut Butter and Jelly.* New York: Dutton.

Westcott, N. (2000). *Skip to My Lou.* Boston: Little, Brown.

ParEnt InvoLveMent ActiVitiEs

IT HAS OFTEN been said that parents are a child's first and best teachers. Without question, parents provide children with the basic foundations on which successful learning experiences can be built. The support, encouragement, patience, and understanding of parents has a profound effect on both the academic and social development of children.

During the first five years of life, when children spend a majority of their time at home, more than 60 percent of their intellectual development takes place. It is during this time that children learn to walk, talk, eat by themselves, develop a sense of independence, and seek to explore the world around them. Children learn more at this time than at any other time in their lives. These foundational skills serve as the basis for the learning and social experiences a child encounters in the more formal atmosphere of the classroom.

The two sections that follow have been designed to provide you with a selection of relevant and meaningful suggestions to share with parents. These activities, in the form of special letters and calendars sent home on a periodic basis, offer parents and other caregivers lively and fun activities that stimulate the development of phonemic awareness.

Letters

This section provides you with several reproducible letters to send home to parents. Each of the letters focuses on direct and easy-to-implement phonemic awareness activities that can be incorporated regularly into the family's daily routine. The suggestions and tips are all proven methods for developing and encouraging successful experiences with the sounds of language.

You are encouraged to send these letters to the parents of your students on a regular basis. Here are a few tips for using the letters effectively:

• Photocopy one letter and sign your name in the space provided at the bottom of the letter. Be sure to add the date at the top of the letter.

• Photocopy the letter in a quantity sufficient for the number of students in your class or in a selected group.

• Send the letter home with your students on a selected day (every other Tuesday or every third Thursday is "Letter Day").

• Encourage students to ask their parents to work with them on the activities and suggestions on each letter. Emphasize that these letters are not "homework" assignments, but rather an opportunity for families to work and learn together.

• You may wish to encourage students to bring in and share selected family activities with other members of the class.

The following strategies may help to facilitate a two-way communication of the letters between home and school:

• Include a letter as part of a regular newsletter/newspaper sent home by the school.

• Clip the letters to school bulletins or homework papers sent home to parents.

• Write a brief, personalized note at the bottom of each letter commenting on something positive about the student.

• Schedule workshops at school at which parents can share some of their favorite phonemic awareness activities, books, or songs.

- Ask the principal or superintendent to prepare a special introductory letter to parents explaining the letters and their value.

- You may wish to have translations of these letters made for parents who don't speak English.

This section (and the one that follows) has been designed to serve as a convenient resource for you as you seek to involve parents in the education of their children. Used throughout the course of your phonemic awareness program, these letters can help ensure that everyone is working toward a common goal and that the best interests of all children are being provided for in an atmosphere of mutual trust, support, and encouragement. The letters that follow include:

Note: The letter on page 173, "Recommended Books," can be duplicated and sent home to parents at the beginning of the school year. You might want to provide the school or public librarian with a copy so that he or she might have the books available, if possible.

Dear Parents:

Our class will be learning many new skills this year. Students will be learning about the sounds in words and how those sounds are blended together. These lessons are part of the reading development of every child, and are important lifelong skills.

I would like to invite you to become a partner in your child's learning experiences this year. I believe your involvement will help your child attain a higher level of academic success. This partnership between home and school can provide your child with a wealth of learning opportunities that will positively affect her or his reading performance.

To help reinforce the work we are doing in the classroom, I will be sending home prepared parent letters and calendars regularly with activities for you and your child to share. These letters are designed to provide you with ideas that can help your child become a successful reader. Each letter and/or calendar contains several choices of activities to share—activities that will reinforce the work we are doing in school without disrupting your family schedule. There are no special materials to buy; no expensive equipment or electronic gadgets are required. Your only investment is a few moments of your time each day—a few moments that can make a world of difference in your child's education.

I look forward to your participation in our learning experiences this year. If you have any questions about these letters or calendars, please feel free to contact me. Let's work together this year to help your child succeed in school!

Sincerely,

Dear Parents:

Reading stories to your children is a most valuable activity. When children listen to adults read, it helps them develop an appreciation for written material and for the ideas and thoughts that books can convey. Many experts in the field of reading have determined that parents who read to their children on a regular basis are more likely to have children who are good readers. Children who have been read to will undoubtedly be eager to read for themselves because they know of the pleasures to be found in books. Here are some suggestions:

1. Before reading to your child, practice reading aloud by yourself the first few times to feel more comfortable.

2. Establish a relaxed atmosphere with no radios, TV, or other distractions. Try setting aside a family reading time when everyone reads.

3. Encourage your child to stop to ask you questions. This shows that your child is interested in what you are reading.

4. You may want to stop from time to time in your reading to ask questions about the characters or events in the story. Ask questions, such as "Why do you think she/he did that?"

5. Be sure to check with the school librarian, the children's librarian at your local public library, and bookstore personnel for suggested books. Provide opportunities for your child to select books she or he would enjoy hearing.

Your child will enjoy the time you spend together. Together we are sending your child on the road to academic success.

Sincerely,

Dear Parents:

Learning to read is one of the most valuable skills your child can ever learn. One practice that helps children on the road to reading success is for parents to set aside a special time each day to read with their children. This sharing time is important since it demonstrates to your child that reading can be fun, exciting, and informative. Best of all, when parents and children share a book together, they have a special time together. Plan to take a few moments each day to share the joy of literature with your child. Here are some ideas:

1. Give your child plenty of opportunities to choose the reading materials to share together. Let her or him pick books based on special interests, favorite characters, or hobbies.

2. Read aloud with lots of expression. You may wish to take on the role of one of the characters in a book and adjust your voice accordingly.

3. As you read an old familiar story to your child, occasionally leave out a word and ask your child to suggest the missing word or another substitute word.

4. Make reading a regular part of your family activities. Be sure to take books along on family outings or trips. Read to your child every chance you get.

Thank you for being an important part of your child's learning. Working together, we can help your child become a great reader.

Sincerely,

Dear Parents:

In order for children to become good readers, they must be actively involved in all the fun and magic of good books. We know that children who are motivated to learn to read are those who are surrounded by the fun of reading. When children know that reading can be a fun, enjoyable, and satisfying activity, they will be actively engaged in all of the skills and activities designed to help them on the road to reading success. Just as important is the fact that children will develop positive attitudes toward reading and learning in general when parents share some fun reading-related activities. Try these motivators:

1. Take lots of photographs of your child with books–for example, taking a book off a shelf, sharing a book with another family member, or looking at a book in a bookstore. Paste these on sheets of paper and ask your child to suggest titles for each one. Then display them.

2. After you and your child finish reading a book together, create a puppet or model of one of the characters. These can be displayed on top of the bookcase or refrigerator.

3. After you have read a book to your child, ask her or him to tell you a word from the story that they especially liked. It can be a funny word, a sad word, a rhyming word, or a strange word. Write the word on an index card and place the card inside the front cover of the book. The next time you share the book with your child, talk about the word on the card and why your child selected that word after the previous reading.

4. Invite your child to draw an illustration or picture of her or his favorite character or favorite part of the story. Be sure these are posted on the refrigerator or family bulletin board.

The time you spend with your child is important. Thank you for all your contributions.

Sincerely,

Dear Parents:

Children need to grow up in a home that is rich in language. Children who have been talked to and who are given opportunities to play with the sounds of language begin to develop language skills that will last their whole lives. It is important for you, as a parent, to spend some time sharing the fun that can be had with words in a variety of learning games and activities. Children need to understand that learning about words and playing with those words can help form a solid foundation for later academic success. One of the best ways to help your child learn about words and their sounds is through a wide variety of rhyming books, games, and activities. Here are a few to get you started:

1. Read Dr. Seuss books to your child on a regular basis. Check with the children's librarian at our public library or the librarian here at school for recommended books. Listening to Dr. Seuss will help your child appreciate the fun that can be had with words.

2. Every day play a quick rhyming game with your child. Listen carefully to words your child says and then create some words that rhyme with your child's words. For example, your child might say, "I played at the park." You might say, "I played in the dark." Your child might say, "Look at the cat." You might say, "Oh, look at that." Be sure to keep this activity playful and fun.

3. Invite your child to point to objects around the house. Ask your child to say the name of the object. Then make up or say a word that rhymes with that object. For example, if your child points to a table, you might say, "Mable." If your child points to a chair, you might say, "Pair." If your child points to a spoon, you might say, "Moon." Again, this should be a playful and fun time.

4. For lots of fun, play a "Silly Name" game with your child. Every time your child says someone's name, try to come up with a silly rhyming name for that person. For example, if your child says, "Are we going to Aunt Brenda's?", you might say, "Yes, we're going to Aunt Tenda's." Your child might say, "Where is Michael?" You might say, "Where is Like-el?"

Learning activities such as these are important to your child's success as a reader. Together we can help ensure a lifetime of reading enjoyment for your child.

Sincerely,

Dear Parents:

In school we are learning about the sounds that letters make and how those sounds can be put together to form words. This is important for children because it helps them learn about all the sounds in the English language and how some of those sounds can be combined to make words. Most important, children learn that one sound or two sounds or more can be put together to create words. As children learn about the sounds in words, they begin to understand the wide variety of sounds there are. You can help your child learn about word sounds with some of the activities and games below. As always, keep the emphasis on *fun*—be sure your child knows that making sounds and learning about sounds can be a playful and enjoyable way to spend a couple of minutes with you.

1. As you read a book or story with your child, look for words that begin with the same letter—for example, two words that begin with *b*. After you've read the story, ask your child a question, such as, "What sound do you hear at the beginning of these two words from the story—*boy* and *bird?*" or "What sound do you hear at the beginning of these two words from the story—*man* and *many*?" Just ask your child for the sounds at the beginning of each word, not the names of the letters.

2. Play a "word pair" game. With your child, locate objects in or around your house that begin with the same sound—for example, "I see a table and a tree," or "I see some green grass," or "I see a carpet and a cat." Invite your child to note the matching beginning sound for each pair of words.

3. As you read a book with your child, invite her or him to listen for words that begin with a pre-selected sound. For example, you might say, "Today, let's listen for words that begin with the /s/ sound," or "As we read this story, let's listen for words that begin with the /t/ sound."

4. Introduce your child to rhythm by having her or him clap to the beat of a favorite song or tune. Demonstrate to your child how each "clap" of the hands stands for one beat in the music. You may want to begin with a song your child knows, such as "Happy Birthday." Here's how you might demonstrate it: "Hap (clap) py (clap) birth (clap) day (clap) to (clap) you (clap).

Spending time with your child is important. Your contributions are important to your child's future reading success.

 Sincerely,

Dear Parents:

As children grow up, they naturally look to adults for guidance. Often children develop their own habits and personality based upon what they see parents and other adults do. For example, a child who sees a parent read a great deal will be inclined to want to read too. Setting a good example involves more than just reading to your child every day. It also involves a measure of encouragement and respect for your child as she or he grows up. You can contribute greatly to your child's reading development through some of the following practices:

1. Give your child lots of praise as she or he learns new skills in school. A little praise each day can go a long way toward building successful students.

2. Don't compare your child with others in the family or in the neighborhood. Respect your child as an individual and allow her or him to grow in her or his own way.

3. Listen to your child and encourage her or him to talk with you. Ask your child to share parts of her or his day with you on a regular basis.

4. Be patient. Remember that growing and learning both take time. Try not to rush your child into something she or he may not be ready to do.

5. Read regularly to your child. After reading, make a comment to your child, such as, "Wow, that was an interesting story!" or "I really enjoyed reading that book to you!" or "I'm glad we had this time to share together."

I appreciate the time you spend with your child. Together we can make a difference.

Sincerely,

Dear Parents:

One of the most valuable skills your child can learn is that of listening. In fact, more than 50 percent of what your child will learn in school will depend on how well she or he is able to listen and follow directions. Young children need to be able to understand, remember, and act on what they hear, both at home and when they are in school.

You can help your child develop good listening skills through some of the following activities. Use some every day as you and your child learn and play together.

1. Read to your child on a regular basis. Point to words as you read them aloud. This helps your child understand the relationship between spoken and written language. As you read, omit a word and let your child suggest one that makes sense.

2. Take time to listen to your child patiently and without interruption. Share the events in your day (at home or at work), using the terms *first, next, last, before,* and *after.* Ask your child about her or his day by using these sequence words. For example, you might ask, "What did you do *first* today?" or "What came right *after* lunch?"

3. As you make requests of your child, note the number of directions she or he can recall and respond to correctly. Make a game of gradually increasing the number of directions she or he can follow. Let your child make up directions for you to follow as well.

4. From time to time, take a walk with your child around the neighborhood or block. Ask her or him to listen for various sounds and to identify them. You may wish to make a recording of the sounds you hear on your walks or around the house.

5. Play a rhyming game with your child. Say two rhyming words to your child and ask for one more word that rhymes with the first two. For example, if you say "hop, mop," your child could say "top." Read nursery rhymes or rhyming poems, leaving out alternate rhyming words. Let your child complete the rhymes as you pause.

I hope you and your child enjoy the time you spend together. I look forward to your continued involvement.

Sincerely,

Dear Parents:

Learning about the world in which your child lives will be a very valuable part of her or his academic and social growth. The concepts your child forms now will serve as the foundation for further exploration and discovery. Opening up the limitless possibilities for learning now can be one of the most valuable things you can do as a parent. You may wish to consider some of the following activities and ideas for you and your child to share together.

1. Talk about size differences with your child. Discuss who is the tallest or shortest person in the family. What is the widest or narrowest item in the living room? What is the lightest or heaviest object in the kitchen?

2. Discuss the position of various objects. For example, what is on your child's left side? Right side? Overhead? Underneath? Behind? In front?

3. Ask your child to look for items in the neighborhood that could be grouped into various categories. You might ask, for example, "What items, like cars, provide transportation?" Responses could include trucks, buses, motorcycles, scooters, skates, and so on.

4. Play a riddle game with your child. Say, "I'm thinking of something that you eat with and it rhymes with *moon*" or "I'm thinking of something that's in your room and it rhymes with *head.*"

5. Give your child some old magazines or newspapers. Work with her or him and cut out pictures of objects similar to those found in your home: table, chair, bed, dresser, and so on. Glue these onto sheets of construction paper and gather them together into a book. Encourage your child to share the book with other family members.

The time you spend with your child is very valuable. Thank you for all of your participation.

Sincerely,

Dear Parents:

At this stage in your child's growth and development, every day is a new day of learning. One important skill is the recognition of various patterns and rhythms that occur around us every day. Learning about patterns and rhythms is an important pre-reading skill because it alerts your child to the fact that words, too, have patterns and rhythms that are similar as well as different. Children learn to appreciate the sounds of words and how those sounds are combined to create new words with some of the following activities. Plan to share these with your child on a regular basis.

1. Work some jigsaw puzzles with your child. Start off with a simple puzzle containing a few pieces, and as your child becomes more proficient, move up to puzzles with more pieces. Give your child opportunities to select puzzles for the two of you to work on.

2. Using several common household objects, such as buttons, beans, pennies, or straws, play a pattern game with your child. For example, line up a button, two beans, and a spoon. Ask your child to duplicate the pattern. Repeat this activity using a variety of patterns. Provide opportunities for your child to set up patterns for you to duplicate as well.

3. Give your child a large assortment of different-sized objects, such as a collection of buttons or a handful of various beans. Ask your child to sort the objects according to size.

4. Play a rhythm game with your child using a selection of different sounds. For example, clap your hands twice, stamp your feet once, and clap your hands twice. Ask your child to repeat the pattern and then to create one for you to copy. You may wish to use kitchen items (spoons, glasses, and so on) to create rhythms for your child to duplicate.

5. Read some nursery rhymes to your child. Ask your child to identify the words that sound alike (rhyme). You may wish to print some of these words for your child.

Thank you for your time and involvement in your child's learning. Together we are making a difference in your child's academic progress.

Sincerely,

Activity Calendars

These reproducible calendars provide families with a wealth of exciting and fun phonemic awareness activities to do at home. There are words to rhyme, sounds to learn, and a host of pleasurable sharing experiences between parents and their youngsters. All in all, there is something for everyone!

Please note that there are some "blanks" for each month. This allows you an opportunity to write in some of your own activities (prior to reproducing the calendars) for parents and children to share. Select certain activities from this book, another teacher resource book, your school/district reading curriculum, a professional publication, or your own imagination. Or you may want to write in "Free Time" in some of these blank spaces to allow families an opportunity to select or create their own word-play activities.

In distributing these letters to parents, make sure they understand that the emphasis is on fun and informality—not on turning the home into a school-away-from-school; in short, these activities are not meant as "homework assignments." Suggest to parents that there are a wide variety of possibilities here for fostering good parent-child interactions while stimulating the development of appropriate phonemic awareness abilities. Parents should have the option of choosing as many of the suggested activities as their schedules and available time allow. Obviously, the more these activities become a regular part of the daily routine of the family, the more they will have an impact on the child's appreciation of oral language.

Dear Parents:

You can help promote a lifetime of reading enjoyment and success for your child by making reading a habit early in her or his life. Sharing the joys of good books and children's literature should be a regular family activity—one practiced every day. You can help your child get into the reading habit by using the following calendar. Post it on the family bulletin board or refrigerator for all to see. Plan a special time each day when you and your child can share a book or story together. Put your child in charge of "recording" each day's reading time with a mark or sticker in the appropriate spaces on the calendar. If you and your child read together for at least 20 days during the month, celebrate the occasion with a special treat or trip. Make another calendar for the following month and keep the reading habit going.

1. Put a check mark, star, funny face, or sticker in a box for each day you and your child read together for at least 15 minutes.

2. You may wish to write in the dates for this month.

3. At the end of the month, invite your child to post the calendar on the refrigerator or some other appropriate place. Later, these calendars can be gathered together in a special notebook.

4. Try to read with your child for a minimum of 20 days each month. This will help establish the reading habit—one that will last a lifetime.

Sincerely,

Family Read-Aloud Calendar

Sunday	Monday	Tuesday	Wednesday	Thursday	Friday	Saturday

Rhyming & Alliteration

Sunday	Monday	Tuesday	Wednesday	Thursday	Friday	Saturday
Share a Dr. Seuss book with your child.	Look around the house: How many things can you find that rhyme with *back*?	Ask your child: Which of the following word pairs rhyme: *bear–share, heat–cat, mole–pole*?		Share a poem by Jack Prelutsky with your child.	Sing a song to your child. Place an extra emphasis on the words that rhyme. Invite your child to do the same.	Listen to a song by Raffi with your child.
Share a Dr. Seuss book with your child.	Try to find two rhyming words on a box of breakfast cereal.	Look around the house. How many things can you find that rhyme with *bug*?	Share a poem by Jack Prelutsky with your child.	Ask your child: Which of the following word pairs rhyme: *ride–game, boat–float, pick–chick*?		Play a game with your child: Invite your child to say a word. You say another word that rhymes. Repeat several times.
Share a Dr. Seuss book with your child.	Listen to a song by Raffi with your child.		Ask your child: Which of the following word pairs rhyme: *fin–mink, ham–wham, sill–thrill*?	Take a walk with your child. Invite your child to point to different objects. For each one, create a matching rhyming word.	Look around the house. How many things can you find that rhyme with *bail*?	Share a poem by Jack Prelutsky with your child.
Share a Dr. Seuss book with your child.		Take your child to the grocery store. Point out some rhyming words on food labels.	Point to a word in the newspaper and make up another word that rhymes. Invite your child to repeat both words.	Look around the house. How many things can you find that rhyme with *lice*?	Listen to a song by Raffi with your child.	Ask your child: Which of the following word pairs rhyme: *cot–plot, best–west, slid–squid*?
Share a Dr. Seuss book with your child.	Share a poem by Jack Prelutsky with your child.	Ask your child: Which of the following word pairs rhyme: *dive–five, fry–nice, bank–skate*?	Look around the house. How many things can you find that rhyme with *dock*?	Visit a pet store. How many rhyming word pairs can you and your child create together (*dog–frog, cat–sat, pet–set*)?	Point to a part of your body (head, toes) and say a word that rhymes (*bed, rose*). Invite your child to repeat what you do and say.	Work with your child to create words (real or make-believe) that rhyme with the names of family members.

Word Parts

Sunday	Monday	Tuesday	Wednesday	Thursday	Friday	Saturday
Share a favorite book together.	What are some words that begin with the sound of f?	How many words can you and your child find that begin with the same sound as dog?		Ask your child to put the following words together to make a new word: cow + boy, snow + man, bird + house.	With your child, clap the number of syllables in these words: baseball, basketball, soccer.	How many words can you and your child find that end with the same sound as cat?
Share a favorite book together.		What are some words that end with the sound of b?	How many words can you and your child find that begin with the same sound as tape?	How many words can you and your child find that end with the same sound as floor?	What are some words that begin with the sound of h?	
Share a favorite book together.	How many words can you and your child find that end with the same sound as top?	What are some words that begin with the sound of n?	With your child clap the number of syllables in these words: pepper, salt, sugar.	Ask your child to put the following words together to make a new word: book + mark, sun + set, play + time.		How many words can you and your child find that begin with the same sound as bear?
Share a favorite book together.	With your child clap the number of syllables in these words: table, oven, carpet.	How many words can you and your child find that end with the same sound as grass?	What are some words that end with the sound of k?	How many words can you and your child find that begin with the same sound as man?		What are some words that begin with the sound of r?
Share a favorite book together.	How many words can you and your child find that begin with the same sound as snake?	Ask your child to put the following words together to make a new word: rocket + ship, rail + road, drug + store.	How many words can you and your child find that end with the same sound as tree?	What are some words that end with the sound of n?	Ask your child to help you put some sounds together to make new words.	What are some words that begin with the sound of v?

Sound Positions

Sunday	Monday	Tuesday	Wednesday	Thursday	Friday	Saturday
Share a Bill Martin book with your child.	Read three words from a piece of junk mail. Have your child tell you the ending sound for each word.	Ask your child: "What sound do your hear at the beginning of these words: *best, bear, bake?*"	Read three words from a cereal box. Have your child tell you the beginning sound for each.	Ask your child: "What sound do you hear in the middle of these words: *bead, seed, feed?*"	Ask your child: "What sound do you hear at the end of these words: *cat, bat, sat?*"	
Share a Bill Martin book with your child.	Ask your child: "What sound do you hear at the end of these words: *map, lap, tap?*"		Ask your child: "What sound do you hear in the middle of these words: *tip, sip, slip?*"	Read three words from a book. Have your child tell you the ending sound for each word.	Ask your child: "What sound do your hear at the beginning of these words: *sell, sleep, safe?*"	Read three words from a can of vegetables. Have your child tell you the beginning sound for each.
Share a Bill Martin book with your child.		Ask your child: "What sound do your hear at the beginning of these words: *tape, team, Texas?*"	Read three words from the comics. Have your child tell you the ending sound for each word.	Invite your child to say a word with the same ending sound as *fly.*	Ask your child: "What sound do you hear in the middle of these words: *made, laid, shade?*"	Ask your child: "What sound do you hear at the end of these words: *sell, spell, tell?*"
Share a Bill Martin book with your child.	Read three words from the newspaper. Have your child tell you the beginning sound for each.	Ask your child: "What sound do you hear in the middle of these words: *rub, sub, stub?*"	Ask your child: "What sound do you hear at the end of these words: *far, car, star?*"		Invite your child to say a word with the same ending sound as *sheep.*	Ask your child: "What sound do you hear at the beginning of these words: *man, map, Mars?*"
Share a Bill Martin book with your child.	Invite your child to say a word with the same ending sound as *chick.*	Read three words from a magazine. Have your child tell you the ending sound for each.		Ask your child: "What sound do you hear at the end of these words: *fly, bye, sky?*"	Ask your child: "What sound do you hear in the middle of these words: *cone, pole, phone?*"	Read three words from a letter. Have your child tell you the beginning sound for each.

Sound Separation

Sunday	Monday	Tuesday	Wednesday	Thursday	Friday	Saturday
Share a favorite book together.	Sing a song with your child.	Invite your child to tell you the number of sounds in these words: *dog, cat, hen.*	Invite your child to show you a word with three sounds.	Look on a cereal box and find a word with two sounds.	Invite your child to tell you the number of sounds in these words: *nose, leg, arm.*	
Share a favorite book together.	Look on a magazine cover and find a word with two sounds.	Invite your child to show you a word with three sounds.		Invite your child to tell you the number of sounds in these words: *at, so, it.*	Sing a song with your child.	Invite your child to tell you the number of sounds in these words: *sun, moon, star.*
Share a favorite book together.	Invite your child to tell you the number of sounds in these words: *one, two, three.*	Sing a song with your child.	Invite your child to tell you the number of sounds in these words: *dot, cub, gum.*	Look on a package of vegetables and find a word with two sounds.		Invite your child to show you a word with three sounds.
Share a favorite book together.		Look on a tube of toothpaste and find a word with two sounds.	Invite your child to show you a word with three sounds.	Invite your child to tell you the number of sounds in these words: *four, five, six.*	Sing a song with your child.	Invite your child to tell you the number of sounds in these words: *mom, dad, lad.*
Share a favorite book together.	Invite your child to tell you the number of sounds in these words: *in, to, my.*	Invite your child to show you a word with three sounds.		Look on a bottle and find a word with two sounds.	Invite your child to tell you the number of sounds in these words: *jeep, peep, keep.*	

Sound Manipulation

Sunday	Monday	Tuesday	Wednesday	Thursday	Friday	Saturday
Share a Dr. Seuss book with your child.	Take away the first sound in *hit* and replace it with a *b*.	Invite your child to take off the beginning sound in these words: *cat, dog, horse, flea.* What sound is left in each case?	Take away the last sound in *bug* and replace it with a *t*.	Invite your child to say the following words without the *t*: *heat, cat, date.*	Invite your child to say the following words without the *b*: *bird, band, bad.*	
Share a Dr. Seuss book with your child.	Invite your child to say the following words without the *d*: *dad, made, bad.*	Take away the middle sound in *cat* and replace it with a *u*.	Take away the first sound in *hat* and replace it with a *f*.	Invite your child to say the following words without the *d*: *dam, dive, dock.*	Take away the last sound in *tap* and replace it with an *r*.	Invite your child to take off the beginning sound in these words: *head, foot, toe, nose.* What sound is left in each case?
Share a Dr. Seuss book with your child.	Take away the last sound in *dock* and replace it with a *g*.	Invite your child to say the following words without the *m*: *map, made, marry.*		Take away the first sound in *gate* and replace it with a *m*.	Invite your child to say the following words without the *k*: *make, take, lake.*	Take away the middle sound in *fog* and replace it with an *i*.
Share a Dr. Seuss book with your child.	Invite your child to take off the beginning sound in these words: *sofa, lamp, table, desk.* What sound is left in each case?		Invite your child to say the following words without the *s*: *pass, lass, mass.*	Take away the last sound in *gum* and replace it with a *t*.	Invite your child to say the following words without the *s*: *some, sing, silly.*	Take away the first sound in *bell* and replace it with an *s*.
Share a Dr. Seuss book with your child.	Take away the last sound in *met* and replace it with an *n*.	Invite your child to say the following words without the *h*: *hose, heavy, heat.*	Take away the middle sound in *clock* and replace it with a *u*.	Invite your child to take off the beginning sound in these words: *wind, rain, puddle, damp.* What sound is left in each case?	Take away the first sound in *mop* and replace it with a *t*.	Invite your child to say the following words without the *n*: *tan, fan, ran.*

Dear Parents:

Following is a list of books highly recommended for children in prescho[...] and first grade. These books have been selected on the basis of their ap[...] children's interests and represent a wide range of award-winning and frequently cited books for this age level. Plan to visit the public library or your child's school library regularly and make these suggestions part of your child's reading adventures and explorations.

Ackerman, Karen. *Song and Dance Man.* New York: Knopf, 1988.

Ahlberg, Janet and Allan. *Each Peach Pear Plum.* New York: Penguin, 1978.

Aliki. *We Are Best Friends.* New York: Greenwillow, 1982.

Bang, Molly. *Ten, Nine, Eight.* New York: Greenwillow, 1983.

Bennett, David. *One Cow Moo Moo.* New York: Henry Holt, 1990.

Bogart, Jo Ellen. *Daniel's Dog.* New York: Scholastic, 1990.

Borden, Louise. *Caps, Hats, Socks, and Mittens.* New York: Scholastic, 1992.

Brown, Marc. *Arthur's Baby.* New York: Joy Street Books, 1987.

Brown, Margaret Wise. *Baby Animals.* New York: Random House, 1989.

Bunting, Eve. *Happy Birthday, Dear Duck.* New York: Clarion, 1988.

Carle, Eric. *Do You Want to Be My Friend?.* New York: Harper, 1971.

Carle, Eric. *The Very Busy Spider.* New York: Philomel, 1985.

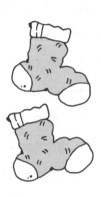

Carle, Eric. *The Very Hungry Caterpillar.* New York: Philomel, 1969.

Carlson, Nancy. *I Like Me!.* New York: Viking, 1988.

Carlstrom, Nancy. *Jesse Bear, What Will You Wear?.* New York: Macmillan, 1986.

Christelow, Eileen. *Five Little Monkeys Jumping on the Bed.* New York: Clarion, 1989.

Cohen, Miriam. *When Will I Read?.* New York: Greenwillow, 1996.

Crews, Donald. *Freight Train.* New York: Greenwillow, 1978.

Crews, Donald. *Parade.* New York: Mulberry, 1986.

Degan, Bruce. *Jamberry.* New York: Harper, 1983.

dePaola, Tomie. *The Popcorn Book.* New York: Holiday House, 1978.

dePaola, Tomie. *Tomie dePaola's Mother Goose*. New York: Putnam, 1988.

Ehlert, Lois. *Feathers for Lunch*. San Diego: Harcourt Brace, 1990.

Emberley, Barbara. *Drummer Hoff*. New York: Simon and Schuster, 1987.

Freeman, Don. *Corduroy*. New York: Puffin, 1976.

Galdone, Paul. *The Little Red Hen*. New York: Houghton Mifflin, 1985.

Galdone, Paul. *The Three Bears*. New York: Houghton Mifflin, 1979.

Goodall, John. *The Adventures of Paddy Pork*. New York: Harcourt, 1968.

Gould, Deborah. *Aaron's Shirt*. New York: Bradbury, 1989.

Havill, Juanita. *Jamaica's Find*. Boston: Houghton Mifflin, 1986.

Henkes, Kevin. *Jessica*. New York: Greenwillow, 1989.

Hessell, Jenny. *Staying at Sam's*. New York: Lippincott, 1989.

Hill, Eric. *Where's Spot?* New York: Putnam, 1990.

Hines, Anna Grossnickle. *Daddy Makes the Best Spaghetti*. New York: Clarion, 1986.

Hyman, Trina Schart. *Little Red Riding Hood*. New York: Holiday, 1984.

Hyman, Trina Schart. *Sleeping Beauty*. Boston: Little, Brown, 1977.

Jarrell, Randall. *Snow White*. New York: Farrar, Straus, and Giroux, 1972.

Keats, Ezra Jack. *Louie*. New York: Greenwillow, 1983.

Keats, Ezra Jack. *Pet Show*. New York: Macmillan, 1972.

Keats, Ezra Jack. *The Snowy Day*. New York: Viking, 1962.

Kellogg, Steven. *A Rose for Pinkerton*. New York: Dutton, 1993.

Kraus, Robert. *Leo the Late Bloomer*. New York: Windmill, 1971.

Lane, Megan. *Something to Crow About*. New York: Dial, 1990.

Lester, Helen. *Tacky the Penguin*. Boston: Houghton Mifflin, 1988.

Lionni, Leo. *Frederick*. New York: Pantheon, 1966.

Littledale, Freda. *The Elves and the Shoemaker*. New York: Scholastic, 1992.

Lobel, Arnold. *Fables*. New York: Harper and Row, 1980.

Lobel, Arnold. *Frog and Toad Are Friends*. New York: Harper, 1970.

Lobel, Arnold. *Mouse Tales*. New York: Harper, 1972.

Marshall, Edward. *Fox on Wheels*. New York: Dial, 1983.

Marshall, James. *George and Martha Rise and Shine*. Boston: Houghton Mifflin, 1976.

Martin, Bill, Jr. *Brown Bear, Brown Bear, What Do You See?*. New York: Holt, 1967.

Mayer, Mercer. *A Boy, A Dog, and a Frog*. New York: Dial, 1967.

Mayer, Mercer. *There's a Nightmare in My Closet*. New York: Dial, 1968.

McPhail, David. *The Bear's Toothache*. Boston, MA: Little, Brown, 1972.

McPhail, David. *Something Special*. Boston: Little Brown, 1988.

Numeroff, Laura Joffe. *If You Give a Mouse a Cookie*. New York: Harper and Row, 1985.

Ormerod, Jan. *Moonlight*. New York: Puffin, 1983.

Ormerod, Jan and David Lloyd. *The Frog Prince*. New York: Lothrop, 1990.

Ormondroyd, Edward. *Broderick*. Boston: Houghton Mifflin, 1984.

Oxenbury, Helen. *Family*. New York: Wanderer, 1981.

Pearson, Tracey. *Old MacDonald Had a Farm*. New York: Dial, 1984.

Peet, Bill. *Merle, The High Flying Squirrel*. Boston: Houghton Mifflin, 1983.

Peppe, Rodney. *The House That Jack Built*. New York: Delacorte, 1985.

Pizer, Abigail. *It's a Perfect Day*. New York: Lippincott, 1990.

Potter, Beatrix. *The Complete Adventures of Peter Rabbit*. New York: Puffin, 1984.

Rockwell, Anne. *My Spring Robin*. New York: Macmillan, 1989.

Seuss, Dr. *One Fish, Two Fish, Red Fish, Blue Fish*. New York: Random, 1976.

Sharmot, Marjorie. *I'm Terrific*. New York: Holiday House, 1988.

Spier, Peter. *Peter Spier's Rain*. New York: Doubleday, 1982.

Spier, Peter. *Noah's Ark*. New York: Doubleday, 1992.

Viorst, Judith. *The Good-Bye Book*. New York: Atheneum, 1988.

Watson, Richard. *Tom Thumb*. San Diego: Harcourt Brace, 1993.

Zolotow, Charlotte. *William's Doll*. New York: Harper and Row, 1976.

Sincerely,

PhonoGrams and LetteRs

ap	ail
ain	ake
ale	ame
an	ank

ap	ash
at	ate
aw	ay
eat	ell

zzzzzzzzz eeeeeeee mmmmmm

est	ice
ick	ide
ight	ill
in	ine

ing	ink
ip	it
ock	oke
op	ore

zzzzzzzz eeeeeeee mmmmmm

ot	uck
ug	ump
unk	

a	b	c
d	e	f
g	h	i

zzzzzzzz eeeeeeee mmmmmmm

j	k	l
m	n	o
p	q	r

s	t	u
v	w	x
y	z	

WORd FaMilies LisTs

THE FOLLOWING 37 PHONOGRAMS can be found in approximately 500 primary-grade words. These phonograms can be used in a wide variety of phonemic awareness activities, particularly in Stage 1. Here are just a few possibilities:

• Select two words from a column. Create a sentence using the two words ("Melissa had a sack on her back."). Invite children to tell you the two words that rhyme (sound the same).

• Print a selected phonogram on an index card and place it in a pocket chart. Using a variety of letters, place each one in the chart in front of the phonogram. Read each word to children and invite them to note the similarities.

• Select one word from a column. Invite children to create a real or made-up word that rhymes with the original word.

• Make up a sentence using a word from a selected word family. Say the sentence to students. Then say it again, omitting the selected word. Invite children to tell you the missing word.

• Say two words (two from the same column or two from different columns). Invite children to touch their ears if the two words rhyme. Invite them to touch their mouth if the two words are different.

• Select several words from one column (specifically, words that can be illustrated, such as *bell*, *well*, and *shell*). Print each one on an index card. On the reverse side of each card, draw a simple illustration of the word. Show a word to students and say the word aloud. Flip over the card (showing the illustration) and invite children to repeat the word to you. Do this several times for maximum effect.

• Copy the following poem, "Teddy Bear," onto chart paper. For each verse invent a second sentence using a word from one of the word families. Then replace the second word in each rhyming pair with a blank. Read the poem to children and invite them to suggest a rhyming word to fill in each blank.

Teddy Bear, Teddy Bear,
Found a ring.

Teddy Bear, Teddy Bear,
Will you _____.

Teddy Bear, Teddy Bear
In the Spring

Teddy Bear, Teddy Bear
Likes to _____.

Teddy Bear, Teddy Bear
Saw some string.

Teddy Bear, Teddy Bear
Has an arm, not a _____.

- Provide each child with a sheet of paper and invite them to fold the paper in half. Read the words from one column to the class. Invite each child to each select two words from the list and draw an illustration of one word on one side of the paper and an illustration of the other word on the other side of the paper.

- Read the words from one column to the children. Invite children to look through old magazines and select pictures of one or more objects that illustrate one or more words from the list. These can be cut out and posted on a Word Family bulletin board.

- Tell children that you are going to take them on a "Sound Safari." Say a word from one of the word families and invite children to find an object in the room that rhymes with the word you said. For example, "I say *fight*. What do you see that rhymes with *fight?*" (*light*) "I say *bone*. What do you see that rhymes with *bone?*" (*phone*).

- Create a deck of index cards with at least ten pairs of words from two separate word families. Mix up the cards and place two randomly chosen cards in a pocket chart. Read the two words to children and invite them to tell you if they rhyme or not.

The number of activities you can create with these word families is virtually limitless. Use these lists as opportunities to demonstrate the fun and playfulness that can be part of any phonemic awareness program.

-ack	-ail	-ain	-ake	-ale
back	bail	gain	bake	bale
Jack	fail	main	cake	dale
pack	hail	pain	lake	gale
rack	jail	rain	make	hale
sack	mail	brain	rake	kale
tack	nail	chain	take	male
black	pail	drain	wake	pale
clack	rail	grain	brake	sale
crack	sail	stain	flake	tale
quack	tail	train	shake	vale
shack	wail		snake	
snack	frail		stake	
track	quail			
	snail			
	trail			

-ame	-an	-ank	-ap	-ash
came	ban	bank	cap	bash
fame	can	rank	gap	cash
game	fan	sank	lap	dash
lame	man	tank	map	gash
same	pan	blank	nap	hash
tame	ran	clank	rap	lash
blame	tan	crank	sap	mash
flame	van	flank	tap	rash
	plan	plank	clap	sash
	scan	spank	flap	clash
		thank	slap	trash
			snap	crash
			trap	splash

-at	-ate	-aw	-ay	-eat
at	fate	caw	bay	beat
bat	gate	jaw	cay	heat
cat	late	law	day	meat
fat	mate	paw	gay	neat
hat	plate	raw	hay	seat
mat	skate	saw	jay	treat
pat	state	draw	lay	wheat
rat		straw	may	
sat			pay	
vat			ray	
flat			say	
that			way	
			stay	
			pray	
			bray	
			tray	

-ell	-est	-ice	-ick	-ide
bell	best	dice	kick	hide
sell	jest	lice	lick	ride
fell	nest	mice	pick	side
sell	rest	nice	sick	tide
well	vest	rice	tick	wide
shell	west	price	wick	bride
smell	chest	slice	brick	glide
spell	quest	spice	chick	pride
		twice	quick	slide
			slick	
			stick	
			thick	
			trick	

-ight	-ill	-in	-ine
fight	bill	fin	dine
light	dill	kin	fine
might	fill	pin	line
night	gill	tin	mine
right	hill	win	nine
sight	mill	chin	pine
tight	pill	grin	vine
	sill	skin	
	will	spin	
	chill	thin	
	drill	twin	
	frill		
	grill		
	skill		
	spill		
	still		
	thrill		

-ing	-ink	-ip	-it
king	link	dip	bit
ring	mink	hip	fit
sing	pink	nip	hit
wing	rink	sip	kit
bring	sink	tip	lit
cling	wink	chip	pit
sling	blink	drip	sit
sting	drink	flip	wit
swing	stink	grip	grit
thing	think	ship	knit
spring	shrink	skip	quit
string		slip	skit
		trip	slit
		whip	split

-ock	-oke	-op	-ore	-ot
dock	poke	hop	ore	cot
lock	choke	mop	core	dot
rock	smoke	pop	score	hot
sock	spoke	top	store	lot
clock	stoke	chop	chore	not
flock	stroke	drop	shore	pot
knock	broke	shop	sore	rot
shock		stop	bore	tot
smock			fore	knot
stock			gore	plot
			more	spot
			lore	trot

-uck	-ug	-ump	-unk
buck	bug	bump	sunk
duck	dug	jump	dunk
luck	hug	dump	bunk
puck	jug	rump	drunk
suck	mug	hump	punk
tuck	rug	lump	plunk
chuck	tug		
cluck	drug		
stuck	plug		
truck	slug		
struck	snug		

Rhyming Picture CaRds

dad

sad

bag

flag

fan

man

map

trap

bat

rat

bed

sled

bell

jet

net

190-198
2 copies of
each page.

brick

stick

pig

twig

chin

twin

king

swing

ship

hip

sock

clock

dog

log

mop

stop

pot

knot

duck

truck

bug

rug

gum

drum

cut

nut

mail

nail

brain

train

cake

rake

ZZZZZZzz eeeeeee mmmmmm

gate

skate

meat

wheat

jeep

sheep

feet

street

dime

time

five

hive

boat

goat

cold

gold

hole

pole

bone

phone

hose

nose

cry

fly

bear

bee

bird

cat

cow

deer

dog

duck

ZZZZZzz eeeeeeee mmmmmm

fish

fly

frog

goat

moose

mouse

owl

pig

seal

shark

sheep

skunk

snail

snake

squid

whale

Two Syllable
AniMal PicTure CaRds

chicken

dolphin

donkey

eagle

giraffe

lion

lizard

monkey

panda

rabbit

raccoon

spider

tiger

turkey

turtle

zebra

Web Sites

THE FOLLOWING WEB SITES can provide you with valuable background information, a wealth of resources, scores of up-to-date lesson plans, and numerous tools for expanding your phonemic awareness program. They can become important adjuncts to any reading curriculum and are appropriate for all teachers at the pre-school, kindergarten, and first grade levels.

Note: These Web sites were current and accurate as of the writing of this book. Please be aware that some may change, others may be eliminated, and new ones will be added to the various search engines that you use at home or at school. Rigby is not responsible for the content of any website listed on these pages. All material contained on these sites is the responsibility of the hosts and creators.

http://curry.edschool.Virginia.EDU/curry/centers/pals
This site offers classroom teachers tons of information and loads of innovative lessons. Developed by the University of Virginia, this site is focused on a statewide program of phonemic awareness activities and procedures targeted to all primary level students. This is a site worth checking out.

http://www.kidsource.com/kidsource/content2/phoemic.p.k12.4.html   (Note: *phoemic,* not *phonemic*)
The article on this site, "Phonemic Awareness: An Important Early Step in Learning to Read" by Roger Sensenbaugh, defines phonemic awareness, explains why it is so important in the reading process, and describes several teaching methods. There are lots of references and good background information in this piece.

http://www.csusm.edu/Quiocho/pa.html
"Reading Instruction Portfolio: Phonemic Awareness Description" is a ten-page article that focuses on the nature and importance of phonemic awareness in the reading development of young children. Particular attention is paid to second-language-learner considerations. Teaching ideas and lots of resources are also included.

**http://teams.lacoe.edu/documentation/classrooms/
patti/k-1/teacher/assessment/levels.html**

This brief article describes the various levels or stages of phonemic awareness from Awareness of Rhyming Words (ages 3–4) to Phoneme Manipulation (age 7+).

**http://www.geocities.com/Wellesley/Atrium/1783/
PhonemicAwareness.html**

Lots of information and activities highlight this 12-page article, which offers teachers a multitude of ideas about what phonemic awareness is and how to teach it. This is an excellent place to start and is written by a teacher for teachers.

http://www.reading.org/positions/phonemic.html

This brief article is a summary of a position statement of the International Reading Association on phonemic awareness and the teaching of reading. Good background information on the value of phonemic awareness is included.

**http://www.ed.gov/databases/ERIC_Digests/
ed400530.html**

This informative site offers an overview of phonemic awareness and its relationship to the "Great Reading Wars." Also included are recommendations for instruction as well as a list of selected references.

**http://teams.lacoe.edu/documentation/classrooms/
patti/k-1/activities/phonemic.html**

Lots of lessons and tons of dynamic activities can be found on this site. Developed by a classroom teacher and geared for fellow teachers in grades K and 1, this site overflows with a wealth of practical ideas.

Abo**U**t the **A**u**T**hor

TONY IS A NATIONALLY RECOGNIZED reading expert well known for his energetic, fast-paced, and highly practical presentations for strengthening elementary education. His dynamic and stimulating seminars have captivated thousands of teachers from coast to coast and border to border—all with rave reviews! His background includes extensive experience as a classroom teacher, curriculum coordinator, staff developer, author, professional storyteller, and university specialist in children's literature.

Not only is Tony an advocate for the integration of children's literature throughout the elementary curriculum, he is also the author of more than a dozen highly acclaimed children's books including *Elephants for Kids* (NorthWord Press), *Slugs* (Lerner), *Cannibal Animals* (Watts), *Exploring the Oceans* (Fulcrum), and *Zebras* (Lerner). With more than 30 years as a professional educator (17 years as a classroom teacher and reading specialist), Tony is currently a professor of education at York College in York, Pennsylvania. There, he teaches elementary methods courses in reading, language arts, science, and social studies. Additionally, he maintains a children's author Web site—http://www.afredericks.com—specifically designed for classrooms and schools across the country.

NoTes

Notes

will say it very slowly. For each sound you will stand behind an individual child seated on the chairs. For example:

The word is *dog*:
- You say /d/ (while standing behind the first child in the row).
- You say /o/ (move and stand behind the second child in the row).
- You say /g/ (move and stand behind the third child in the row).

The word is *card*:
- You say /k/ (while standing behind the first child in the row).
- You say /ar/ (move and stand behind the second child in the row).
- You say /d/ (move and stand behind the third child in the row).

Hint: This activity works particularly well when children have an opportunity to select several words from a book being read to them. Invite them to suggest some words and then select several one-syllable (three- or four-phoneme) words from the list they dictate.

Variation: As the children become familiar and comfortable with this activity, invite one to stand with you behind the row of seated individuals. Stand behind the child and place your hands on her or his shoulders. Help that child move with you as you say a selected word. Invite several individuals to participate in this physical segmentation activity.

12 Invite the entire class to stand up. Tell the children that you will say some words to them, one at a time. Instruct them to place both hands on the sides of their heads when they hear the first sound in each word. Tell them to place both hands on their waists when they hear the middle sound in each word. Tell them to put their hands on their feet when they hear the ending sound in each word. (*Note:* This activity requires the use of three-phoneme words only.) Here are some examples:

Book: /b/ (hands on head); /oo/ (hands on waist); /k/ (hands on toes)
Cake: /k/ (hands on head); /a/ (hands on waist); /k/ (hands on toes)
Tub: /t/ (hands on head); /u/ (hands on waist); /b/ (hands on toes)
Pig: /p/ (hands on head); /i/ (hands on waist); /g/ (hands on toes)

13 Provide several small teams of children with four small inexpensive bar magnets each. Tell the children that you will say a word and that they are to repeat it back to you. As they repeat the word, they are to place a magnet on a table for each sound they hear in the word. For example, you say *baby*. Children repeat the word and:

- Place one bar magnet down for the /b/ sound.
- Place another bar magnet down for the /a/ sound.
- Place a third bar magnet down for the /be/ sound.

Invite the children to repeat each target word by sweeping a finger across the magnets, touching each one as each sound in the word is said. This activity works best with two-, three-, or four-phoneme words selected from a nursery rhyme or children's book.

Note: This activity is quite instructive because as children put down each magnet, the magnets will be attracted to each other (depending on their polarity). Children begin to see how sounds are "attracted" or "linked" to each other to form units we know as words.

14 Draw a picture of a train locomotive, several passenger cars, and a caboose on a sheet of construction paper (or trace the following illustration). Cut out the individual objects and put a small hook and loop fastener dot on the back of each one. Place the corresponding hook and loop fastener on the chalkboard or a large sheet of oaktag on which you have drawn a train track.

Tell the children to listen carefully to a word you say and to watch as you place a part of the train on the board or sheet of oaktag. Tell them that you will place the locomotive on the board when you say the first sound in a word. You will place a passenger car (one or two) after the locomotive for the middle sound(s) in a word. And, you will place the caboose on the board for the ending sound in a word.

Variations:

- Invite the children to repeat each word with you. At the same time, point to each train car to identify the first, middle, and ending sounds in the target word. When the children are comfortable with this procedure, reverse the activity and remove the locomotive as you say the first sound, the passenger car(s) as you say the middle sound(s), and the caboose as you say the ending sound.

- Invite individual children to come to the front of the room. Say a target word and encourage a child to place each train car on the board to represent the beginning, middle, and ending sounds of the word.

- Prepare sufficient quantities of the train cars so that each child in the class has a collection. Repeat the activity above, inviting all the children to participate at the same time.

15 **D**raw and cut out several paper fish from a sheet of construction paper. On one-third of the "fish," write the number 1. On another third, write the number 2. On the final third of the "fish," write the number 3. Place a small piece of magnetic tape on the back of each "fish."

Provide selected individuals in the class with a straw onto which has been tied a magnet on a length of string. Spread the magnetic fish over the top of a table or desk. Tell the children that they are going on a fishing trip with you. You will say a target word. Invite a child to use her or his "fishing pole" to pick up one of the "fish" on the table. Have the child check the number on the "fish" and to say the sound from the target word corresponding to its position in the word. For example, the target word is *duck*:

• Say the word *duck.*

• Invite a child to pick up a "fish."

• Encourage the child to say the number on the "fish" (for example, 1).

• Invite the child to say the middle sound in the target word (the number 2 represents the middle sound; 1 is the beginning sound; and 3 is the ending sound).

• The child will say /u/.

Here's another example:

• Say the word *tree.*

• Invite a child to pick up a "fish."

• Encourage the child to say the number on the "fish" (for example, 1).

• Invite the child to say the first sound in the target word.

• The child will say /t/.